The Beauty of Indoor Plants

Today indoor gardening is a hobby that fascinates young and old, busy and retired, homeowner and apartment dweller. Ferns and palms and many other conservatory plants now thrive at windows. New possibilities regularly appear in growers' catalogues. You can select from 3000 orchids, 1500 bromeliads, 1400 begonias, 700 gesneriads and an unbelievable number of others—enough to keep you enchanted for several lifetimes. You can have handsome foliage subjects and colorful flowering plants, even miniatures. Some are dramatic, others have a delicate, lacy charm. Take thought before you buy; a large plant is expensive, an investment almost like a piece of furniture. Well-cared-for, it can be as much a part of your home as a chair or table.

Certain plants are particularly appropriate for certain settings. The dwarf orange-tree from China is Oriental in character. Amaryllis and lycoris offer vivid color, resplendent on coffee table or in a hall. Anthuriums with satiny leaves are stunning and deserve a special place. If you have high ceilings, select a schefflera tree or a stately ficus.

Ornamental caladiums look nice almost anywhere. They are not too large nor to small. Hibiscus and oleander are large and need a corner to themselves where they sing with color when they bloom.

A special growing area such as a sunroom or a bright bay window offers a fine opportunity for flowering plants. But for almost every location with some light, you can find a plant that will thrive. Choose accordingly. Some plants need warmth, others coolness. An orchid from the mountains of Peru will not grow in heat; African-violets from the tropics will not thrive where it is cold.

Place your plants where there is light, water them regularly, and with a minimum of other attention most of them will flourish. If you give them half a chance, they reward you with rich green foliage, lovely flowers in many colors.

Proper selection is vital for success; culture is important. But what you put where is the key to success. Analyze the conditions you have to offer; then buy accordingly.

Here, then, is a guide to the selection and care of indoor plants, whether in your home, in a small office, or in the large lobby of a public building. In this book, you will find your old favorites, popular standbys, new imports—the choice is vast—1000 plants to decorate your rooms, to enrich your life.

Jack Kramer

January 1968

Chicago, Illinois

Contents

Illustrations

In Black and White

In Line

1000

BEAUTIFUL

HOUSE PLANTS

and How to Grow Them

I

Attractive Ways with Plants

One plant on a window sill is attractive, but a group of them—an indoor garden—makes a picture. And here it is easy to water and care for each one. The garden can be part of a room or it can fill a sun porch, a bay window, or more often today, a plant room. Living plants bring charm and freshness to any area.

Before you start, decide where the growing area will be and consider what conditions you are going to have for plants. Certainly, choose them for their beauty but also for their suitability. Some plants need warmth, others coolness; some grow in sun, others thrive in semishade; all need light to some degree.

Garden rooms and sun porches

Years ago a conservatory, garden room, or sunroom was built for plants and it was also a place to enjoy morning coffee. Today we are witnessing a revival of the plant room. Here ideal conditions prevail whether in the sun porch of an old house or the atrium of a new one, and plants flourish. There is ample light, adequate warmth, and humidity. The selection of plants for these areas is almost limitless. You can choose from among palms, ferns, begonias, camellias, and geraniums; you can have some small trees in tubs; you can enjoy standard heliotrope and lantana, to mention a few. Special equipment is not necessary and having the garden in one place makes it easy to care for.

Many plants come from the tropics but this does not mean they must be smothered in warmth; in fact, they prefer cool, but never freezing, nights. An unheated room is a great place for an indoor garden. I have a pantry with a south window where cool-growing orchids grow lavishly. It is like a small conservatory, a pleasant retreat off the kitchen. Don't overlook the possibilities of unheated but enclosed porches or storerooms for plants.

1 A window garden for Helen Van Pelt Wilson's entrance hall.
Gottscho-Schleisner photo

2 A sunny stairway decorated with plants in boxes and on brackets.
Roche photo

Window gardens and window greenhouses

Plants grow well in window gardens if there is light and a good circulation of air. They make pretty silhouettes against the glass and they bring the outdoors indoors. Even one shelf of plants makes a window something more than an opening in the wall, and glass shelves, which let light pass through, are easy to keep bright and clean. Putting them up is a simple business, and you can buy them with the brackets at most hardware stores.

A metal planter with plants on the sill may become another garden. Sheet-metal shops make them to size for you, or you can buy plastic or fiberglass boxes. These cost less and require little maintenance. They come in various sizes to fit windows and in pastel colors that blend with most furnishings. An ideal length is 36 inches. This accommodates seven 5-inch pots. If you are growing only a few small plants, you might prefer fiberglass trays. They come 2 to 3 inches deep and in various lengths. Neat and easy to clean, they look very nice.

You can also enjoy plants in a minature window greenhouse, an outside rather than an inside garden. Prefabricated units come knocked-down for you to assemble. Although it is not the easiest task in the world, it is worth the effort because

3 Decoration for Lois Wilson's hall with a shining green peperomia featured in a copper-gilt container, a handsome tray behind it, and in front a pair of horses' heads. Panda photo

window greenhouses are ideal for almost all plants. Units come in four sizes (see list of suppliers at the end of this book).

These greenhouses have tops and sides of glass; the house window makes the fourth side. A convenient size for some twenty plants is 20 inches deep by 32 wide by 22 high. Snow and rain drains off the slanted roof.

Artificial light gardening

Where there is not enough window space or where light is poor, closets, attics, and basements can be made into gardens by means of artificial light. African-violet enthusiasts were among the first to discover this, and they have turned many a cellar into a lovely indoor garden. For plants growing under lights, plastic trays can be purchased in various sizes and colors or galvanized tin can be bent to specifications by a tinsmith.

Electric supply stores carry appropriate fixtures. If you want a commercial unit, you can buy a table or floor model from one of the mail-order specialty houses listed under Sources of Supplies at the end of this book. Most readily available units are equipped with two or four fluorescent tubes. Some have facilities for installing incandescent bulbs along with the tubes. Twenty-four or 48-inch fluorescent tubes are convenient for apartments or homes. Table models come with adjustable light canopies; floor models consist of movable carts fitted with shelves.

The visible spectrum, like a rainbow, has colors ranging from red to violet. Plants require blue, red, and far-red light waves to produce normal growth. Blue enables them to manufacture carbohydrates. Red controls the assimilation of these, and also affects photoperiodism, their response to relative hours of light and darkness. Far-red is one of the spectrum colors that affects plant growth; it has an elongating affect on stems and increases leaf size; it can also inhibit seed germination. Quite possibly, yellow also plays a part in the growth of plants. Although we still do not know all the ways light affects plants, we do know that the best sources of artificial light for indoor gardening are fluorescent and incandescent lamps.

Standard fluorescent lamps—cool white, warm white, daylight, and natural white—emit red and blue waves. Cool white has the best balance of red and blue for plant growth but contains no far-red waves. Most fluorescent lights are designed to produce high levels of red and blue but have little if any far-red. However, Sylvania's Wide-Spectrum does have the far-red and a little more of the yellow-green, and therefore does not give the purple glow usually associated with growth tubes.

Wherever it is possible to install them, the most efficient fluorescent tubes will be the 8-foot lengths which are 72 to 75 watts. The 40-watt tubes come in 4-foot lengths. Since efficiency of all fluorescent tubes falls off 2 inches from each end, one 8-foot tube is more economical than two shorter ones. The 8-foot tube has only two ends of poor light or 4 inches loss against the four ends of two 4-foot tubes, or 8 inches

5

4 An orange-fruited Jerusalem cherry, a fine Christmas gift plant, on a vermilion stand for a large living-room table. Roche photo

5 A handsome, but easily-grown, aglaonema in a floor planter.
Hort-Pix photo

7

6 A cheerful breakfast corner in Helen Van Pelt Wilson's house with philodendron in a hanging basket, grape-ivy and an ivy geranium on a double bracket, and on the table, a small-leaved English ivy trained to a trellis and set off by a woven container. *Home Garden* photo

loss. But anyone who can do simple arithmetic can more accurately determine the requirements of his own particular growing area. An easy formula consists of a minimum of 20 watts of illumination per square foot of growing area. This would be applicable to the list of plants given below with the plant tops about 8 to 10 inches from the lights.

While plants are classified as long-day, short-day, and day-neutral, it is really the period of darkness that the plant pigment phytochrome measures. Species vary in their phytochrome sensitivity, and this sensitivity is also affected by temperature. Thus long-day plants like the begonia come into bloom when nights are short. Short-day plants flower with long periods of darkness. If temperatures suit them, day-neutral plants, given adequate light for the manufacture of food, will bloom regardless of the hours of dark and light. But a long stretch of darkness is so vital to some plants that light from a street lamp 25 feet away will inhibit their bud formation. Among these are the Christmas begonia, Christmas cactus, chrysanthemum, gardenia, morning glory, and poinsettia, none of which is for the beginner in artificial light gardening.

The criteria for photoperiods can be determined by increasing or decreasing the half-day (12-hour) period. Most house plants are long-day (short-night) photoperiodic and therefore require a night of *less* than 12 hours.

Proper temperature is also a factor in success with artificial lights. From growing orchids in natural light, I know that cymbidiums and many coelogynes will not bloom at a night temperature of 65F; they need it cooler, 55F or less. However, light intensity determines response to low temperatures. With more light, my outdoor cymbidiums in California bloomed freely with 42F at night, but cymbidiums indoors at 52F with less light, matched them in flowers. Light intensity, light duration, and night temperature work together in determining bloom or vegetative growth. With orchids, each kind is apparently individual in its needs.

Gardening under artificial light is a challenge and specific plant-by-plant information is beyond the confines of this general book. However, the cultural directions given for more than a thousand plants apply whether you are growing them under natural or artificial light. Follow these, and then you might refer to a book entirely devoted to gardening under lights, as *Fluorescent Light Gardening* by Elaine C. Cherry (D. Van Nostrand Company, Princeton, N.J.) or *Gardening Indoors Under Lights* by Frederick H. and Jacqueline L. Kranz (Viking Press, New York, N.Y.). You can also get a wealth of information and a good magazine if you join the Indoor Light Gardening Society of America, Inc. (The membership secretary is Mrs. Fred D. Pedan, 4 Wildwood Road, Greenville, South Carolina 29607.)

Because plants grown under artificial light never experience cloudy days, smog, or air pollution, they manufacture the sugars important to growth at a high steady rate. Gray winter weeks do not keep them almost dormant like your window plants in such weather. To maintain the accelerated rate of photosynthesis, you must provide plants under lights with sufficient water and fertilizer, giving somewhat weaker solution more frequently than recommended, thus providing steady availability of food for the manufacture of sugars. When watering, use tepid water. Foliage on plants under lights is often damaged when cold water is used.

In general, until you have experience with plants under lights, you will be wise to grow those that will thrive in temperatures comfortable to you, always provided *there is about a 10-degree drop at night*. This is easy to manage since most heating units are controlled by a thermostat, and you can simply set this lower at night before you go to bed. Here then is a list of plants, all of which have been successfully grown under artificial light.

Some Plants to Grow Under Artificial Lights

Abutilon	Fittonia
Anthurium	Geraniums
Aphelandra	Gesneriads (especially African-violets)
Begonia	Kalanchoe
Browallia	Lantana
Cactus	Palms
Caladium	Peperomia
Camellia	Philodendron
Campanula	Prayer-plant (Marantha)
Coleus	Roses (particularly miniature)
Crassula	Rosary-vine
Dieffenbachia	Shrimp-plant
Dracaena	Spider-plant
Euphorbia	Tradescantia
Ferns	Velvet-plant
Ficus	Wax-plant

Lobbies and offices

Offices and lobbies of public buildings are usually display areas. To make these attractive, to soften the sometimes severe lines of brick, marble, stone, and glass, interior designers select growing plants and, as a rule, large specimens. Built-in planters are an aspect of architecture today, and lush green foliage plants and flowering ones, too, make clients and visitors feel welcome. Bromeliads and ferns are perhaps the most popular, although dieffenbachias, rubber trees, and philodendrons are also favored. Because bromeliads fare so well in lobbies, they are becoming known as "institutional plants."

To make plants thrive as long as possible, proper planting is important. A rich, porous soil and adequate drainage arrangements are vital, along with routine care. Designers planning groups should select compatible plants. Shade-tolerant philodendrons, ficus, and schefflera are one good association; dracaena and podocarpus, another. The fine sculptural qualities of New Zealand flax and others of this phormium species look well almost anywhere. Flowering plants, chrysanthemums, cyclamens, and lilies offer bright seasonal color and can be replaced with other budding plants as these are offered by florists through the year.

Container plants in offices and showrooms have indeed become commonplace and tall specimens like the Queensland umbrella-tree, *Schefflera actinophylla*, often appear in luxuriant condition. Whether from a rental service or grown by an employer, plants are an attractive decoration for a place of business and there are kinds for every light exposure. The finest office specimens I have seen were a supposedly

7　A window greenhouse accommodates a bright collection of flowering and foliage plants.

8　A commercial cart for growing plants under artificial light. Tube Craft photo

delicate tree, *Ficus benjamina*—thriving beside a vice president's desk—camellia trees blooming in a New York showroom, and standard roses ablaze with color in a doctor's waiting room.

All growing things need care, and those in institutions are no exception for they must always be on display. While we might expect that living plants would not thrive in public buildings, ironically, they often grow better because they receive better care there than those grown in the home.

2

Pots, Planters, and Baskets

Selecting containers for plants is a pleasure. Although many of the ceramic jardinieres and urns are attractive, you will probably want only a few as accents, and perhaps a pedestal urn or decorative pot to compliment an interior. For the majority of plants, I prefer standard clay pots. They look nice, are inexpensive, and plants thrive in them.

Pots, clay or plastic

Standard clay pots in sizes from 2 to 24 inches in diameter are suitable for most plants. (Pot sizes are always measured by diameter not depth.) The shallow azalea pot or bulb pan is better for begonias, many orchids, and other plants with scant root systems. Large Italian pots with rounded edges are most attractive, especially for camellias and citrus trees. To set off bulbs or desert plants like an agave or echeveria, the new, three-legged, shallow clay pots are excellent.

Plastic pots have the advantage of being lightweight, easy to handle, easy to clean, and almost unbreakable. Furthermore, they do not promote the growth of algae. They come square or round, deep or shallow, with or without the conventional band, but size is limited to a 10-inch diameter.

It is a good idea to buy the proper-sized clay saucers along with the pots. Most saucers now have a protective coating. This prevents water from seeping through to stain table top or other surface.

Tubs and planters

Square or tapered tubs of redwood are fine for large plants. The wood lasts for years and needs no preservative. Soy tubs and porcelain containers are attractive for plants of delicate appearance; jardinieres put a specimen plant on display. Glazed ceramic tubs, although handsome, usually have no drainage holes. I do not recommend them for direct planting for I have lost too many plants due to accumulation of mois-

15

9 An attractive floor planter equipped with fluorescent lights.
U.S.D.A. photo

ture, and proper watering is just too much of a problem. I prefer to slip a potted plant along with a saucer into a ceramic tub rather than risk the fatality of undrained, soggy soil.

A large tub with a big plant in it is heavy. For this, buy a commercial dolly, and put it under the tub. Then you can move it about easily as health or decoration indicates.

Built-in planters can be pleasure or pain, depending on size and placement. If they are too large they take so many plants the cost is high and care is time-consuming. Committees for churches and public buildings have sometimes discovered this to their sorrow and, in a few instances, have actually boarded up all or some of their planters.

As a room-divider, newly filled, a planter can indeed be attractive, but in any location without overhead light, few plants survive, let alone flourish, more than a month or so. Periodic replacement is therefore necessary. Floor-to-ceiling windows offer a fine location for planters. Whether set at floor level or recessed in the floor, they break the monotony of a solid window wall, and also serve as a guard rail in front of the glass. Planters at each side of an entrance welcome guests and, if there is a skylight in the hall, exotic ferns and palms thrive in them with colorful flowering specimens—chrysanthemums, poinsettias, and lilies—introduced from time to time.

Planters made of wood require galvanized insert pans. Your local sheet-metal shop will make these for you. Specify a turned lip; otherwise sharp edges are a hazard. Or insert plastic liners in planters.

You can grow plants directly in the soil of a planter or, if you prefer, leave plants in pots and place them on a layer of stones. Cover the top soil with sphagnum. If you plant directly in soil, add charcoal to it to help keep it sweet, and water with the greatest care. Let the soil get almost dry before you water again. Without bottom drainage, soil in planters easily becomes a soggy mess.

Hanging baskets

Containers suspended at windows put plants in a favored position for light and air. Basket plants add color to bare walls, and leaves and blossoms are mostly at eye-level where they can be fully appreciated. If growing space is limited, say, to one window, basket containers suspended from the ceiling offer additional display.

Nurseries and florists carry a variety of hanging containers of wood, wire, clay, and plastic. Some have clip-on saucers so no drip pans need be placed on the floor. Furthermore, plants can be watered in place and trips to the sink avoided.

Redwood baskets are good for fuchsias, ferns, and begonias, as well as many other plants. Wood retains the moisture that keeps roots cool, and the containers last for years. Open wire baskets are inexpensive and in them in summer, achimenes, campanulas, and columneas become cascades of color. Ivy geraniums and episcias are a lovely sight in clay baskets. Plastic containers are good where fast loss of moisture poses a problem.

Most baskets come with wires, chains, or ropes for hanging. But you must supply a ceiling hook that will adequately support the weight of a basket of plants with moist soil. Use heavy-duty eye-bolts, screw eyes, or clothesline hooks.

Culture in baskets

It is easy to grow basket plants because so many good conditions are going for them. Roots benefit from air circulation, drainage is assured, and soil does not become stagnant.

Before planting, line a slatted redwood or open-wire basket with sphagnum moss. Press it firmly against the sides. Then fill in with soil suited to the species you are growing and group plants according to their needs. A haworthia that likes to be grown dry will not succeed in a basket that must be kept moist enough for ferns; shade-loving orchids suffer in the sunlight that pleases campanulas and abutilons. For attractive basket plantings, place an accent plant in the center, and fill in and around it with such trailers as episcias and achimenes.

In open wire baskets, soil dries out quickly and plants need water once a day in summer, sometimes twice, much less often the rest of the year. Suspend baskets at a convenient height, then you can water them in place with a long-beaked watering can.

Some Favorite Basket Plants

For sun

Abutilon	flowering-maple
Achimenes	rainbow-flower
Asparagus sprengeri	asparagus-fern
Begonias	(many types)
Browallia	
Campanula	star-of-Bethlehem
Chlorophytum	spider-plant
Columnea	
Episcia	Peacock-plant

For shade

Aeschynanthus	lipstick-vine
Ferns	
Kohleria	
Sedums	stonecrops

18

10 Here plants in a kitchen area bring bright color and warmth into the home. Handsome white ceramic pots are set on a pebble tray. Kentile Corp. photo

3

Your Thriving House Plants

Generally speaking, house plants are of two kinds: those that require cool growing and those that revel in warmth. But every plant needs light and will not grow or even live without it. Some plants thrive at a sunny east or south window, others grow best in a bright western exposure; and many foliage plants make lovely greenery in north light. Select your plants accordingly. Wherever you place them, turn them regularly so that growth will be even and not one-sided as they reach toward the source of light. African-violet enthusiasts even advise a quarter-turn every day!

For many plants, humidity or air moisture of 30 to 40 per cent is adequate, and almost all living rooms provide this much. For species requiring more, humidity can be increased in various ways, and this is discussed later in this chapter. Fresh air is also essential to health, even in very cold weather. Some plants need special care; others grow almost, but never entirely, untended.

Soils

A good potting soil is essential. One part garden loam to 1 part sand to 1 part leafmold is what I use for most plants. For cacti, succulents, and some euphorbias, I allow almost ½ instead of ⅓ sand. I put in peatmoss for the acid-loving azaleas and camellias and also for the anthuriums and tuberous begonias that need a moist condition. Peatmoss is vegetable matter in an arrested state of decomposition. It is free of fungi, rich in carbon. It has a spongelike structure that absorbs and retains ten to twenty times its weight in water. It prevents soil from caking and helps to aerate it. Orchids and bromeliads need osmunda (chopped roots of various ferns) or fir bark (steamed pieces of evergreen bark). Both can be obtained in small sacks at nurseries.

Commercial packaged soil, usually rather "light," is good for some plants, particularly African-violets and begonias, but, if much is needed, it is expensive. A better soil mixture can usually be bought by the bushel from a greenhouse. This will be the same soil used there. It has been sterilized and contains all necessary ingredients.

11 Pittosporum and a ficus tree in an island planter, and a large
patio garden for the contemporary offices of the All Steel Equipment Co., Hedrich-Blessing photo for Frazier, Orr, Rafferty, and
Fairbanks, architects.

22

12 A Norfolk-Island-pine and a large schefflera for green accents in the lobby of an office building. Hedrich-Blessing photo for Architects Associated.

You can use it as is or alter it according to the needs of your own plants. If it is not porous enough, you can add more sand; if it feels thin, put in more leafmold or other humus.

Growing mediums that contain no soil have been developed by Cornell University; they are called peatlite. For one peck, combine:

4 quarts, dry measure, Vermiculite (#2 Terralite)
4 quarts, dry measure, shredded peat moss (German or Canadian)
1 level tablespoon ground limestone
1 level tablespoon 5-10-15 fertilizer

Mix ingredients uniformly. For sowing seeds or transplanting young plants, moisten well. When you shift plants to larger pots, the moistening can be done after plants are repotted.

I have found this medium excellent for seedlings and, because it is lightweight, advantageous for big plants in tubs. If you use it, be sure to give supplemental feeding of a water-soluble fertilizer every other watering through the growing season. Potting procedure with the peatlite mix is the same as with standard soils.

23

13 A built-in planter with daffodils, tulips, narcissus and various green plants; in the background vines and tall plants trained against the wall. Roche photo

In general, garden soils contain weeds, seeds, insects grubs, and bacteria that can cause disease in plants. Sterilizing the soil avoids these hazards. If you cannot buy treated soil, you can sterilize it at home. It is a messy, smelly procedure but it can be done. Put dry soil through a fine sieve into a pan of water; don't pack it. Put the pan on the stove and turn up the heat until the water boils; then simmer for a few minutes. Turn out the soil into a clean baking dish and let it dry out. Or you can bake moistened soil in your oven in a roasting pan for two hours at 200F. In any case, let the soil cool for 24 hours before use.

Although a basic soil bought at a greenhouse suffices for most plants, some prefer less potash, others more nitrogen. It is a good idea to test soil. An inexpensive soil-test kit (from suppliers) will enable you to determine the exact alkalinity or acidity without guessing.

The pH scale indicates the degree of alkalinity or acidity. The scale is divided into fourteen points; neutral is 7.0, indicating that alkalinity and acidity are in balance. Alkalinity is indicated above 7.0 and acidity below 7.0. To maintain the proper level for acid-loving plants, add acid peatmoss or cottonseed meal to the soil or water with a diluted acid fertilizer like Miracid, or about twice a month with vinegar solution, ½ teaspoon to 1 quart of water. To make soil more alkaline, add lime. Here are the pH preferences of some plants:

4.5 to 6.0	6.0 to 8.0
Amaryllis	African-violet
Araucaria	Asparagus-fern
Azalea	Begonia
Cactus	Geranium
Camellia	Oxalis
Coffea	Palm
Dieffenbachia	
Ferns	
Gardenia	
Hydrangea	
Philodendron	

Potting and repotting

Potting refers to the first planting of a seedling or cutting in a container; repotting refers to the transfer of a plant from one pot to another, usually to a larger one. For good growth give plants proper potting. Select a container neither too large nor too small in relation to the size of a specimen.

When potting a plant, be sure of a clean container. Before use, new clay pots should be soaked overnight in water; otherwise they will draw undue moisture from the

POTTING A PLANT

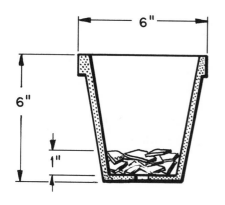

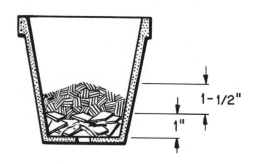

a. USE POT SHARDS OR SMALL PEBBLES FOR DRAINAGE MATERIAL

b. POUR MOUND OF SOIL

c. CENTER PLANT ON MOUND OF SOIL AND FILL WITH SOIL

d. SECURE PLANT BY PACK-ING SOIL, LEAVING 1" ON TOP FOR WATERING

soil of new plantings. Old pots should be well scrubbed with steel wool soap pads and hot water to remove any accumulation of algae or salts. In some areas where the water is full of chemicals, the accumulation of salts on pot rims may be so difficult to remove that it is necessary to discard the pots.

Fit an arching piece or two of broken pot (shards) over the drainage hole. Over the crocking, spread some perlite or porous stones with a few pieces of charcoal, the charcoal to keep the soil sweet. Then place the plant in the center of the pot and fill in and around it with a fresh soil mixture. Hold the plant in position with one hand; fill soil in and around it with the other. Firm soil around the stem with your thumbs. To settle the soil and eliminate air spaces, strike the base of the pot on a table a few times. A properly potted plant can be lifted by the stem without being loosened.

Leave about an inch of space at the top between pot rim and soil to receive water. Water newly-potted plants thoroughly; then for a few days keep them in a light rather than a sunny place. Once accustomed to brightness, they can be moved. Label all plants; it's nice to know what you are growing.

When roots push through the drainage hole in a pot or appear on the surface, it is time to give more root room and also to replenish the soil. An exact schedule for repotting is not possible; instead, consider the needs of each plant. If you fertilize regularly, thus replacing soil nutrients, plants thrive in the same pot longer than if they are not fed.

To check the condition of roots and the possible need for a larger pot, hold your hand over the soil (it should be slightly moist), keeping the main stem between your fingers. Invert the pot and knock the rim sharply against the edge of a shelf or table. Rap the base also. The whole rootball will then drop easily into your hand. If it is covered with a network of roots, the plant needs a larger pot, but rarely more than an inch larger in diameter.

Sometimes examination of a poor specimen will indicate a partially rotted root system or inadequate roots for the size pot in which the plant struggles to survive. Then the need is for a smaller not a larger pot; in a smaller pot, a somewhat sickly plant may show surprisingly quick recovery. In any case, when you shift a plant to a smaller or larger pot, crumble away as much old soil as possible and replenish with fresh.

Specimens in very large containers, more than 14 inches across, or in permanent planters, as room dividers, are best left undisturbed as long as possible. To recondition them, dig out 3 to 4 inches of surface soil and replace it with a fertile fresh mixture. This process is called "top dressing" plants.

Sometimes it is absolutely necessary to reduce the size of an enormous plant that has outgrown the space you can allow it. This can be done with a strong heart and a sharp kitchen knife. Slice off 3 to 4 inches of the lowest roots and 2 to 3 inches all around the sides. Repot the plant in a smaller more manageable container and water well. The best time for this drastic treatment is in summer with 2 months of agreeable outdoor living before the transfer to indoor quarters. By September, there is usually a

tremendous amount of new growth. This procedure has worked for me with asparagus-fern, dracaena, and gardenia.

Watering and feeding

How and when you water depends on the type of pot used, where you live, and the kind of plant. None should be allowed to go completely dry (even during semi-dormancy), and none should be kept in soggy soil. If soil is too dry, plant roots become dehydrated and growth stops. Continuously wet soil becomes sour and roots rot.

Some plants prefer an evenly moist soil; others, such as begonias and clivias, grow best in soil that is allowed to approach dryness between waterings. Cacti and some other succulents may be permitted to become almost completely dry.

28

When you water, do it thoroughly. Allow excess water to pour from the drainage hole; the complete root system needs moisture. It is harmful if only the top soil gets wet and the lower part stays dry. Then the soil usually turns sour and growth is retarded.

Water of room temperature is best. If possible, water in the morning so the soil can dry out before evening. Lingering moisture and cool nights are an invitation to fungus diseases.

Soaking in a pail of water or at the sink is good for most plants and necessary for large ones with heavy roots. With top watering the deepest roots too often are not thoroughly moistened. Set the pot in water up to the rim for an hour or more until the top soil *feels* moist. Azaleas, camellias, and hydrangeas, philodendrons, rubber plants, and ferns thrive with such treatment. Even if we seem to give these plenty of water, the lowest soil areas are likely to remain dry. With capillary action (drawing water up from below), all parts of the soil are moistened. Of course, this works only for plants in porous pots.

Most plants benefit from feeding; however, bromeliads and such flowering plants as many orchids and also clerodendrum, do not need it. Commercial fertilizers

15 Attractive foliage plants: *Rhoeo discolor, Araucaria excelsa,* and *Pilea cadierei.* U.S.D.A. photo

29

contain some nitrogen, an element that stimulates foliage growth, but too much can retard development of flower buds. Fertilizers also contain phosphorous to promote root and stem development and to stimulate bloom, and potash which promotes health, stabilizes growth, and intensifies color. The ratio of elements is marked on the package or bottle in this order: nitrogen, phosphorous, potash. There are many formulas; I prefer 10-10-5 for most house plants.

New plants and ailing plants do not require feeding. New ones in fresh soil have adequate nutrients and do not need more; ailing plants are not capable of absorbing nutrients. After they flower, allow plants to rest for a few weeks; water only occasionally and do not feed. A safe rule is to fertilize only the plants that are in active growth.

Foliar feeding, applying fertilizer to the leaves in a water solution, is often recommended. However, hairy-leaved plants, such as some begonias and African-violets, objects to lingering moisture on leaves especially if the solution is not of room temperature. My best results have been with commercial soluble fertilizer applied to the soil.

There are dozens of plant foods. As I said, I prefer a commercial, soluble 10-10-5 fertilizer. Contents and recommendations are marked on containers. Do follow the manufacturer's directions.

Heat and humidity

Cool-preference plants, such as, campanulas and hoyas, need 54 to 58F at night, 10 to 15 degrees more during the day. Warm-growers like anthuriums and most begonias, require 64 to 68F at night, 72 to 80F during the day. With few exceptions (indicated in the plant dictionary) most plants fall into one of these groups. In other words, average home temperatures suit most plants.

In winter, it's necessary to protect plants from extreme cold. On very cold nights, put cardboard or newspapers between plants and windows to mitigate the chill of the glass.

Although automatic humidifiers are now part of many heating systems, older apartment houses and buildings do not have this advantage. Humidity—the amount of moisture in the air—should be at a healthful level for both people and plants. A humidity gauge (a hygrometer) registers the amount of relative humidity. Thirty to 40 per cent is average for most homes and good for most plants. However, some, as clivia and philodendron, will grow in low humidity, say 30 per cent; others, as rechsteinerias and gloxinias, require humidity of 70 to 80 per cent.

The difficulty is to keep humidity in proper relation to artificial heat and to summer heat. The hotter it is, the faster air dries out. Because plants take up water through roots and release it through leaves, they give off moisture faster when the surrounding air is dry than when it is damp. If they lose water quicker than they can

16 A handsome pedestal container with philodendron plants. Architectural Pottery photo

17 'Princess Fiat', a double, shrimp-pink geranium, a vigorous grower and particularly good outdoors. This basket, its liner holding four good-sized plants grown from cuttings made in August the year before, decorated Lois Wilson's terrace table from the warmest days of the following spring until fall. Before frost, it was brought in to a sunny window in a cool room. Panda photo

18 Suspended, three-section wall planter with upright and trailing
foliage plants. Architectural Pottery photo

replace it, foliage becomes thin and depleted. When summer heat is at its peak between 11:00 a.m. and 1:00 p.m., spray plants lightly with water. For years, a fifteen-cent window-cleaning bottle for misting plants was essential equipment for me. Now new sprayers on the market give better misting than my old-fashioned gadget. Made under various trade names, the hand-operated fog-maker has a plastic non-corrosive washable container and comes in 16- or 32-ounce sizes. It dispenses a fine mist that is beneficial to almost all plants, cleansing the foliage and, for a brief time anyway, increasing the humidity.

In winter, when artificial heat is high between 6:00 p.m. and 8:00 p.m., provide more air moisture. Turn on your room humidifier then, or mist pots and soil surface but not foliage. At night wet foliage is an invitation to disease.

In addition to misting, set plants on wet gravel in, say, a 3-inch deep, large metal or fiberglass tray. This furnishes a good amount of additional humidity. Plants can also be placed on pebble-filled saucers; keep stones constantly moist. Best of all provide an inexpensive space-humidifier that operates on a small motor, breaking water into minute particles and diffusing it through the atmosphere.

Strong growth and firm leaves (assuming temperature and light are in proper proportion) are signs of good humidity. Spindly growth and limp leaves usually indicate too little moisture in the air. Keep plants away from hot radiators and blasts of hot air, also out of drafts.

Fresh air and air-conditioning

Plants grown in rooms with good air circulation do better than plants in a stuffy atmosphere. It's a good idea to let outside air into rooms where plants are growing. In winter, when artificial heat is used indoors, the air is drier than outside; free ventilation helps maintain desirable humdity. If t is impossible to open windows where the plants are growing, see to it that there is adequate ventilation in an adjoining room. But always avoid admitting air in cold drafts that blows directly on the plants.

Air conditioning is a boon to people in climates where summers are hot. It is interesting to me to see that plants also resent torrid weather. Many house plants like bougainvillea and rhizomatous begonias suffer when temperatures soar. However, I have seen bromeliads and palms in excellent health in public buildings with central air conditioning. While I thought that low humidity that prevails with artificial cooling might harm plants, they did not show signs of poor growth from the lack of moisture in the air. Uniform temperatures seem to be far more beneficial than the hot and cold extremes of summer.

However, cold air from wall or window air conditioners directed at plants can harm them. Drafts have a desiccating affect because they cause excessive loss of moisture. Leaves wilt or turn yellow and fall.

19 Foliage plants in clay pots make a flexible center of interest on shelves of a contemporary room divider. Potted Plant Information Center photo

Seasonal care

A controlling factor of plant growth, indoors and out, is weather. As seasons change so do plant requirements. In spring, new growth begins. Give plants more water then and start a mild feeding program. Repot old plants, prune and trim others. February and March can be the busiest months for the indoor gardener, and this is particularly true if you want a fresh green look for your spring window gardens and later plenty of summer color. Be sure that plants are ready for the warming trend. New soil with adequate nutrients starts them off right. Adequate humidity and regular watering keep them healthy.

In summer, most plants grow rapidly, even indoors. Some, such as columneas and fuchsias, need plenty of moisture at the roots, at least once and, as necessary, twice a day. Feed plants that are in active growth. Protect them from noonday sun which may be too strong now for most of them. Usually a window screen suffices but in the South a thin curtain may be required.

Watch out for pests, and provide good ventilation and humidity. Avoid a stuffy atmosphere. On very hot days, mist plants several times to reduce heat.

Fall brings changing weather—some days hot, some cool—a crucial time for house plants. Water with care, each according to its need. With many of them, as fuchsia, hedychium, oleander, growth has matured by winter and they are in a semi-dormant condition. Stop feeding these; never try to force resting plants to sprout fresh leaves. Let the soil go somewhat dry but not so dry as to get caked.

20 Interesting containers in various shapes and sizes for house plants. Architectural Pottery photo

21   Tall foliage plants for accent in a spacious window garden: *Sansevieria trifasciata*, a variegated *Codiaeum*, and *Fiscus elastica*. U.S.D.A. photo

House plants outdoors

A summer outdoors is beneficial for almost all house plants. It helps them to store up vigor so they will be at their best later indoors. With warmth, natural light, and rain water, they grow rapidly and prosper. Move them out to porch or patio when the weather is warm and settled late in May or June (depending on climate), and bring them indoors soon after Labor Day.

However, some plants, mainly hairy- or soft-leaved species, such as African-violets, gloxinias, ruellias, hirsute and various other begonias are better left inside. They do not react well to increased humidity and periods of high heat. Drying winds and lingering moisture or dew on foliage almost always cause trouble. Big vines, such as bougainvillea and passiflora, are also better not moved. Outside they grow too vigor-ously in warm weather. Sometimes I have had to hack away half a plant because I could not otherwise separate it from an outdoor post or wall.

Of course, house plants are decorative outdoors. Philodendron, grape-ivy, English ivy, vining geraniums, and fuchsias look most attractive in hanging baskets suspended from a porch or pergola beam. They are also a graceful addition to a veranda when they are set on brackets fastened to the house wall. Screened and shaded porches become green gardens with ferns and large foliage plants that have been indoors all year, and these are refreshed by a summer outside in a protected situation. Baskets of sun-loving geraniums and lantanas hanging at the side of an entrance, and pots of carissa, prayer-plant, jasmine and zonal geraniums are a welcome sight grouped beside a flight of wide steps.

Outdoors, assemble the majority of your plants in some protected place, perhaps under a large shrub or an open-leaved tree where wind and rain will not harm them. Stake large plants so they do not tip over in wind. Regardless of location, keep them all in pots. The growing season in most climates is too short to put them in the ground, for when repotting is necessary in fall, roots are sure to be damaged and plants set back just when you want them decorative indoors. Set pots on the ground or sink them in earth up to the rims.

Light is intense outdoors and even sun-lovers can be scorched by a sudden change from house to garden. In fact, only a few plants like geraniums, after gradual conditioning, can endure full sun all summer. I find the best location is along the east or west wall of the house. Having them in one area makes it easier for me to care for them.

Outdoors in summer, give plants routine garden care, water, and spray them lightly with a hose every day except in wet weather. On hot, dry days they may need to be soaked and sprayed twice. I also spray them every three or four weeks with malathion. In periods of torrid humidity, mildew may appear. Dusting with sulfur is one deterrent but never on a day over 8oF or foliage will be burned. Phaltan or Zirneb is also a good mildew control.

Years ago, what to do with plants at vacation time was a problem. Now new devices help water your plants while you are gone. Having plants in wick-fed flower pots is one solution. Moisture is supplied from storage saucers to root systems through fiberglass wicks, or glass wicks are available for converting clay and other pots with drainage holes into self-watering pots. The Floramatic waterer is a glass vial that, filled with water, is inserted in the pot soil and automatically dispenses water to the plant. If these devices are not available in your area, simply water your plants thoroughly and place in plastic sealed bags and set them away from the window, in light but not in sun. Or place pots in a large pan of sand placed in a bowl of water. But if you are going away for more than ten days or two weeks, ask your local greenhouse to board the plants for you or get a plant-sitter to air and water your plants.

When plants rest

A plant is a living organism and like people who sleep to regain energy, plants rest at some time of year, growing more slowly or not at all, and flowering kinds stop setting buds. This dormancy is vital. Many of the plants we grow indoors—orchids,

22 A well-grown palm in a handsome footed white bowl. Architectural Pottery photo

fuchsias, and hypocyrtas—come from climates with sharply defined seasons of rain and drought. Though far removed from their habitat, their cycles of growth remain the same, and we must respect them if we are to be successful.

In general, most plants need less moisture or none at all for a short period at some time of year. Of course, there are exceptions. Some like blue-sage, *Eranthemum nervosum*, must be kept fairly moist all year even though this has a long out-of-bloom period through spring and summer. Many plants rest a little after flowering unless they are kinds that make heavy foliage growth then, as clerodendrums and pentas. Summer-flowering plants, such as achimenes and epiphyllums, have a fairly dormant period in winter. Hardy bulbs, of course, go completely dormant and are left entirely dry for several months; tender bulbs, such as amaryllis, freesia, and zantedeschia, also become dormant. But some plants, given good culture, bloom continuously; the African-violet is one of these. Most geraniums never stop making new growth and buds. Only a few of the species, like *Pelargonium fulgidum*, go fully dormant in summer. Ruellia does not die down but after a long period of fall-to-early summer bloom, it stops growing and sets not a single flower until about October.

Usually plants plainly indicate their need for rest. You will see signs of declining vigor. Unless a plant is suffering from some pest or disease, encourage it to slow down. Gradually reduce watering and, of course, stop fertilizing.

4

Bottle and Dish Gardens

and Standards

Bottle gardens and terrariums have great charm—perhaps it is that they give such a close-up view of nature; perhaps it is our pleasure in creating landscapes in miniature. Almost any glass container will serve, from a sherbet dish to an aquarium. And there are hundreds of miniatures of larger flowering plants—African-violets, begonias, cyclamens, fuchsias, geraniums, orchids, and roses—as well as many tiny foliage beauties like the English ivy 'Star'. Most appealing is the minute *Sinningia pusilla*, the miniature gloxinia, with tiny lavender flowers.

Bottle gardens and terrariums

To plant a sizable glass garden, first make a rough sketch of the landscape you want. Then put in soil and mound it into hills and valleys. Place a few stones and select one of the tiny ground-covers, such as *Pilea microphylla*, baby's-tears (*Helxine*), or moneywort (*Lysimachia nummularia*). Keep large plants to the rear of the landscape, smaller ones up front. Choose kinds that are naturally small or else grow slowly, and don't fertilize; you want the plants to stay in proportion. Set a piece of glass over the container; lift it briefly once a day to let fresh air circulate inside.

Keep glass gardens out of sun but in bright light. Moisture accumulating on the sides of the glass drips down to freshen the planting. Sometimes it is not necessary to water your diminutive garden for weeks or even months.

Planting takes patience and a steady hand. First polish the inside and outside of the glass. Inside, wipe off any cleaning spray with a lintless cloth fastened to a bent wire. Through a funnel, pour in drainage material, tiny broken pieces of clay pots, and then soil to fill the container about one-third way up.

23 A well-planned terrarium with miniature plants including partridge berry, club and pincushion mosses, pipsissewa, and other tiny woodland plants. Roche photo

With the wire or a stick make holes for roots. Now you are ready to plant. Remove plants from pots, wash soil from roots, and insert plants in the holes with the bent wire. Press earth firmly around the roots.

Dish gardens

A pottery bowl, a bonsai pot, a clay saucer, even a baking tin makes an attractive setting for a dish garden. This can be a little landscape with trees, shrubs, and grass or simply a collection of interesting plants; it can be formal, informal, Oriental, tropical, or contemporary. It can include mountains and valleys, with small plants for trees, or have accents of rocks and figures among the plants. Just one plant and a few well-chosen stones can be effective.

The scale of the garden—the proportion of rocks and plants to each other and to the container—is vital. One out-of-proportion plant can spoil the effect. You might start with some accessory bit, a stone, a piece of fencing, or a figure, and design around it. Your miniature garden can be an imaginative landscape or a small duplicate of some large, outdoor garden. For trees, choose single-stem plants; for shrubs, branching plants. Instead of grass, grow a tiny ground-cover.

Two popular types of dish gardens are the so-called Oriental, with dwarf palms and small azaleas, and the desert with cacti and succulents. I have also seen tropical rain forests and beach scenes ingeniously developed. At local nurseries and in mail-order catalogues, you can locate fascinating plants to stimulate your imagination, and keep your fingers busy. Small plants are usually classified as Miniature to 5 inches, Dwarf to 8 inches, and Small-Medium to 14 inches.

Select a container 3 to 4 inches deep and in keeping with your motif. If you plan a landscape, a container of Oriental design may be best. A tea cup or sherbet dish is good for a simple accent arrangement, as one plant with a few well-chosen stones.

It is essential to group plants that will thrive under the same conditions. For example, aloes, crassulas, echeverias, haworthias, and peperomias require a somewhat dry, sandy soil and full sun. Dwarf palms, some gesneriads, and azaleas need semishade and rich, evenly moist soil.

Water dish gardens less often than house plants for there is no drainage outlet. Keep the soil barely moist and don't feed the plants. Remember you don't want the plants in your dish garden to outgrow it.

Standard plants

Standards—plants grown to tree-form—are not only for garden and terrace. They can also be enjoyed indoors. Acacias, avocados, chrysanthemums, citrus, fuchsias, geraniums, heliotrope, lantana, oleanders, and roses are some of the many plants that lend themselves to this training. Select a suitable container. It will always be on display so perhaps use a decorative tub for direct planting or an attractive jardiniere to hold a pot. Select a flowering or foliage specimen. Fuchsias and oleanders are best for colorful flowers; acacia, avocado or citrus for foliage.

You can train a standard right from a cutting but it does take patience, care, and time to nurture a small piece of tip growth to tall maturity—usually four years for a geranium. It is easier and quicker to start with a well-rooted plant from a nursery. Firmly stake your standard, and give it good culture with consideration for light, temperature, humidity, water, and food. On a young tree, remove all side shoots as soon as they form. In summer, enjoy your standard outdoors where it can benefit from natural air currents and rain.

Most admired are my azalea and chrysanthemum standards that have been outdoors in summer and moved into the house for fall and winter decoration. It is doubtful if you can grow a tree at a window but most certainly it will succeed in a plant room or an enclosed porch. Try one; a well-grown standard is a delight.

Plants for Flowering Standards

AZALEAS
    'Alaska'—large double, pure white
    'Constance'—single, cerise-pink
    'George Tabor'—single, delicate pink

BEGONIAS
    'Corallina de Lucerna'—rosy-pink
    'Ellen Dee'—orange
    'Orange rubra'—orange
    'Thurstonii'—cerise

25   Three glass gardens: in an aquarium, a brandy snifter, and a
berry bowl. Roche photo

FUCHSIAS

'Amy Lye'—single, white tinged with pink
'Beauty'—double, scarlet and rosy magenta flowers
'Flying Cloud'—double, creamy white with a touch of pink
'San Mateo'—double, pink and dark violet
'Stream Liner'—single to semidouble, crimson

GERANIUMS

'Lavender Ricard'—double, lavender-rose white-centered flowers
'Masure's Beauty'—double, rosy-red
'Orange Ricard'—double, orange-to-scarlet
'Will Rogers'—single, vivid purple-crimson

5

Bulbs for Color—

Winter into Spring

The beauty of the hardy bulb is not only in the flowers; bulbs are easy to grow, and with them you can have color indoors from late November until April. Tulips and hyacinths make any winter morning a promise of the spring that is to come. Planting the bulbs in late fall is like burying treasure for the new year. When they burst into bloom some rainy February morning, you'll know what I mean.

The confines of a bulb already hold the makings of roots, leaves, and flowers. After bulbs are potted and in storage, with reasonable care, you are assured of colorful bloom.

Hardy bulbs

Tulips, hyacinths, and daffodils are familiar forcing bulbs. "Forcing" means handling bulbs so that they will bloom indoors well ahead of their natural outdoor season. You can plant bulbs in soil you purchase in bags or you can make your own mixture by combining half a pail of coarse sand with one pail of rich soil, adding a little lime and a 5-inch pot of bonemeal.

I prefer to plant bulbs in pans. These are not so deep as standard pots but deep enough to accommodate the roots of most bulbs. A 5-inch container is good for one daffodil or one hyacinth. An 8-inch bulb pan is large enough for several tulips. Soil should be loose beneath the bulbs to encourage rooting; the soil on top should be firm to keep the developing roots from lifting the bulb. Plant so that the neck of a bulb reaches slightly above the soil line. After potting the bulbs, moisten the soil well.

26 Marian C. Walker's colorful January window of small blue hyacinths 'Borah', early single orange tulips 'De Wet'—both growing in soil—and large blue Dutch hyacinths 'Myosotis' in pebbles and water. Plantings made about October 21 offer this bloom at the end of January. Shemelia photo

Three stages of forcing

Bulbs are ready to be forced in three stages. First, they need a period of cool rooting (40 to 50F) indoors in a cold but not freezing cellar, closet, or garage, or outdoors in a cold frame trench, or window-well. Second, they require brief exposure to moderate warmth (60 to 65F) with some light but no sun. The third and final stage involves moving them to a cool (about 70F) bright window where they can perfect their flowers.

For *indoor* rooting, I put the pots in an unheated pantry where it is 45 to 50F during the late fall months. Planted bulbs are set on shelves in an airy place without light. I keep them just moist. The soil cannot be either soggy or dry during this important rooting time.

To root bulbs *outdoors*, prepare a trench deep and wide enough to accommodate the largest pot. The bottom of the pots should be about a foot below the soil surface. Place the well-watered pots of bulbs in the trench and cover with 2 to 3 inches of sand to keep the new leaves clean. Then fill in between and over the pots with soil to ground-level; spread over all a thick layer of oak leaves, salt hay, or evergreen boughs to prevent freezing. A cold frame with a hinged top is easier to deal with than a trench but be sure it is in a well-drained place. Cover the sunken pots inside with straw or similar material.

As soon as pots are filled with roots—in six to nine weeks depending on the type—bring them to light for the second stage of forcing, in moderate warmth, not

27 Marian C. Walker's window in mid-February. The bright flowers of 'Golden Harvest' and orange 'De Wet' tulips (in the background), the red 'Couleur Cardinal' and more 'De Wet' tulips (in front), with light yellow 'City of Harlem' hyacinths—from October plantings—set off by green house plants of grape-ivy in pots and a bowl of cut pachysandra. Shemelia photo

over 65F. They are ready to move if roots are making their way through the drainage hole in the bottom of the pot. But first give the bulbs from the outdoors a day or two at 50F. Water the bulbs as you do other house plants. Don't fertilize; the embryo flower has already been formed.

For the third stage, before placing the plants to bloom, be sure tulips are up about 4 inches, the stalks of Dutch hyacinth are showing pale color, and that the buds of daffodils are well up and vigorous looking.

After bulbs bloom, if you want to keep them, water the soil until the leaves wither naturally; then after frost, plant the bulbs permanently in the garden. If you don't have a garden, better discard them; it is not possible to force them again. But after one or two years in the garden, they will recover and bloom outdoors as well as new bulbs.

Selection for Forcing

Early Tulips	Late Tulips
'Brilliant Star'	'Fantasy'
'Crown Imperial'	'Rising Sun'
'Scarlet Cardinal'	'Scarlet Admiral'

Early Hyacinths	Late Hyacinths
'Bismarck'	'King of Blues'
'Delight'	'Marconi'
'Dr. Lieber'	

Small bulbs to force

The small bulbs—crocus, grape-hyacinths, and scillas—can also be brought into early bloom indoors. They are treated much the same way as the larger bulbs.

There are many crocus species; perhaps the most popular is the lavender-blue or purple *C. seiberi*. But you might also try one of the fine whites. *C. biflorus* 'White Lady', or the orange *C. aureus*. 'Venus Vanguard', a rosy-violet stays in bloom from Christmas until late January if planted not later than October fifteenth.

Grape hyacinth or muscari is of dwarf habit and produces blue or violet or pure white flowers that are sweetly scented. *M. botryoides* is a good white for forcing and *M. armeniacum cantab*, an excellent blue.

Scillas are dwarf and compact and bear white or blue flowers. The best for indoors is *S. siberica*; if you prefer white, try *S. siberica alba*.

Plant the small bulbs as soon as you get them. Put ten or twelve in a 6- or 8-inch container in the same soil you use for larger bulbs. Place the pots in spahgnum or peatmoss to keep them cool. After dark rooting, bring them in for forcing at 40 to 45F. When leaves are up, move the pots to an airy place at 60F until buds are almost open. Then place pots at your coolest window, out of sun.

50

I AUTHOR'S GARDEN ROOM. Beam-and-glass roof and glass walls make this a perfect place for growing a great variety of begonias, bromeliads, orchids, and many other plants. *Joyce Wilson photo*

II UNDER ARTIFICIAL LIGHT. (Above left) African-violets and other gesneriads thrive under a table fixture. *Robert Wright, Jr. photo for Gesneriad Saintpaulia News.* (Above right) The iron-cross begonia develops fine foliage color and also blooms with extra hours of light. *Park Seed Co. photo*

III SIX STUNNING HOUSE PLANTS. (Facing page, lower left and right)
The zebra-plant, *Aphelandra*, and the Kafir-lily, *Clivia*. (Above left
and right) Bird-of-paradise, Strelitzia, and the glory-bower, *Clerodendrum*. (Lower left and right) Lantanas and *Crossandra*. *Park
Seed Co. photos*

IV   A lovely amaryllis adds color and charm to this indoor setting;
the bloom will last for many weeks. *Author photo*

Bulbs to Grow in Water

Some bulbs, such as Dutch hyacinths, French-Roman hyacinths, and paper-white narcissus grow as well in water as in soil, and there are advantages to this procedure. It's easy to handle bulbs without soil and forcing can take place entirely indoors, in light at about 45 to 60F.

Hyacinths

Start Dutch hyacinths from December first to February fifteenth. Dust off soil from the bulbs and remove any loose skin that might cause rot. Fill a hyacinth glass (available at florists) with water up to the neck and place a bulb in the top section. Keep the water supply up to the base of the bulb but don't cover the neck or the bulb may decay.

Put the glass in a cool dark place at 40 to 45F. Add water to maintain the proper level. Now wait until the bulb has good root growth and foliage, and flower spike are in evidence; six to eight weeks are required. The leaves should be not less than 4 inches before glasses are moved to a bright, but not too warm, room to bloom. These are good forcing hyacinths:

'Grand Maitre'—single blue.
'L'Innocence'—single white.
'Pink Pearl'—single rose-colored.

Here is one of my successful schedules for Dutch hyacinths:
Bulbs planted—December 15
Brought into light—February 8
Showing color—February 10
First floret open—February 11
In full bloom—February 13

French-Roman hyacinths are smaller, often more charming than the Dutch type. The flowers—white, blue, or pink—last longer and they also have a delightful perfume. Bulbs are set in a bowl or similar container and held in place with pearl chips, stones, or vermiculite. Plant bulbs as soon as they are available in the fall. Allow six or seven for an 8-inch container. Keep it in a cool, dark, airy place until the bulbs are well-rooted. (This takes about eight weeks.) Then move them to light (not sun) and grow them cool until buds show. Now move to warmth for bloom. Try these dependable ones:

'Rosalie'—pink, for Christmas.
'Snow Princess'—white, for mid-January.
'Vanguard'—pink, for Christmas.

Wait to start the other reliables for water-growing listed here until early February; some will be in bloom by March.

28 Lois Wilson's late winter picture of forced white 'Cheerfulness' narcissus and purple crocus in a hammered pewter-washed copper box. Panda photo

29 Elements of the planting: the copper box, heavy pinholder with caulking compound to hold it down, groupings of yew and narcissus bound with pipe cleaners and crocus bulbs in flower, with stones for weight and concealment. Panda photo

30   Paperwhite narcissus—the easiest of bulbs to force—in a white bowl filled with stones and water. Burpee Seed Co. photo

Narcissus

There are many kinds of narcissi but probably the easiest to force are the tazetta or polyanthus varieties. The flowers are fragrant and appealing in color—orange-and-yellow, all yellow, or all white, as the familiar paperwhites. Bulbs bloom readily if planted in a bowl of pebbles and water or in a pot of soil. Select a bowl about 3 inches deep and wide enough to hold at least 3 bulbs. Fill the bowl halfway with pebbles and set the bulbs in place with half-an-inch between them. Add more pebbles to cover all but a third of each bulb. Pour water into the bowl until it just touches the base of the bulbs; add more as required to maintain this level.

Now set the container in a cool (50-55F) place for about three weeks until roots are formed. Then move to a bright window where the bulbs will bloom. The time to start paperwhites for Thanksgiving is October 15; for Christmas, November fifteenth. Plantings made at intervals of ten days will give a succession of bloom through winter and spring. Discard bulbs after they flower. The orange-and-white Chinese sacred-lily and golden 'Soleil d'Or' are slower than the paperwhites and better held for February and March flowers.

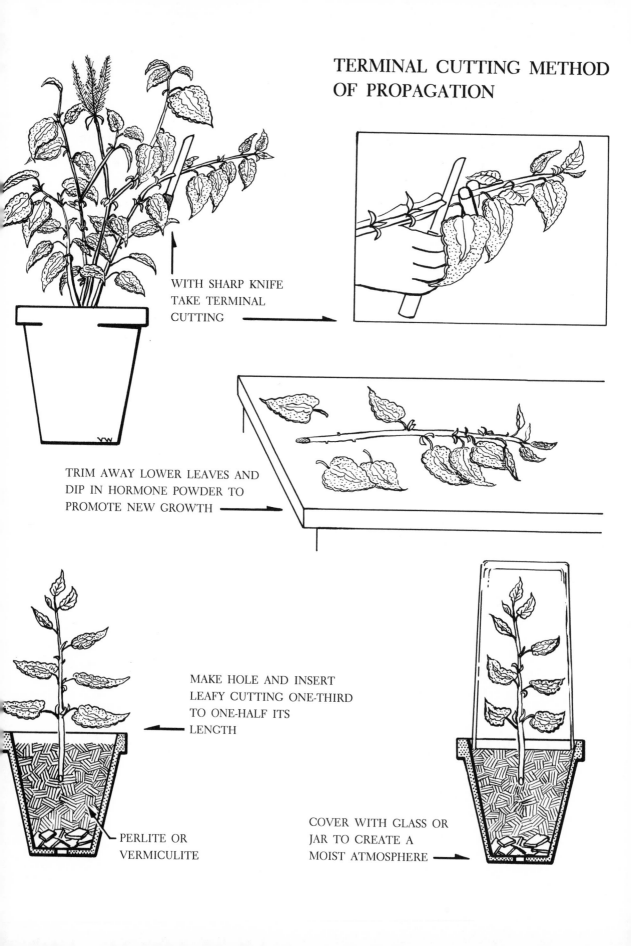

TERMINAL CUTTING METHOD OF PROPAGATION

WITH SHARP KNIFE TAKE TERMINAL CUTTING

TRIM AWAY LOWER LEAVES AND DIP IN HORMONE POWDER TO PROMOTE NEW GROWTH

MAKE HOLE AND INSERT LEAFY CUTTING ONE-THIRD TO ONE-HALF ITS LENGTH

PERLITE OR VERMICULITE

COVER WITH GLASS OR JAR TO CREATE A MOIST ATMOSPHERE

6

Increasing Your Supply

Plants are generous with offspring. In fact, sometimes I hardly know what to do with all my divisions, cuttings, and seedlings. Seeing your own plants grow brings satisfaction and, as with your children, you like your own best. You do not have to be a botanist to propagate plants. It is an easy procedure with many possibilities.

Cuttings—stem and leaf

For stem cuttings, select sturdy shoots, usually in spring. Cut off 4-inch pieces just below a leaf node, the little swelling on the stem. Remove foliage from the lower 2 inches. You can root cuttings of some plants, as rhizomatous begonias, philodendrons, and syngoniums, in a jar of water on the window sill. Others, the majority, as dieffenbachia, tradescantia, and pilea, are planted in vermiculite, sand or other light growing medium, and placed in a warm, humid atmosphere. Breadboxes, baking dishes, plastic dishes, casseroles—any container that has a cover—make good propagating cases. So do bulb pans with glass jars over them. Before planting you can dip the base of the cuttings in hormone powder to stimulate root growth. Then insert them one-third to one-half their length in the propagating mixture. Grow cuttings warm, 75 to 80F, and place them in bright light rather than in sun. Keep the growing medium moist. Lift the cover an hour or so a day to ventilate.

Many plants—rex begonias, African violets, sedums, kalanchoes, and others —can also be propagated by leaf cuttings. Select firm healthy leaves. Make small cuts across the veins with a sterilized knife or razor blade. (Just run it through a match flame.) Lay the leaf on moist vermiculite in the propagating container. To assure contact between leaf and growing medium, weight the leaf with pebbles. Plantlets form at the slit veins and draw nourishment from the mother leaf. When the plants are large enough to handle easily, put them in 2- or 3-inch individual pots.

Propagate large foliage plants, such as alocasias, dieffenbachias, and philodendrons, by cuttings of mature stems, each piece about 4-inches long. Coat both ends with sulfur, lay the pieces in the rooting medium, cover lightly, and press them firmly in place. New plants form from dormant eyes all along the cane.

Stolons and offsets

Many plants produce stolons or runners, among them, chlorophytum, episcia, and neomarica. Take runners about 3 inches long and handle them like cuttings. Roots develop and plants are ready for planting in soil in four weeks to four months, depending on type. Bromeliads, many orchids, gesneriads, and agaves develop offsets or suckers at the base of a mature plant. When these are 2 to 4 inches long, cut them off with a sterile knife, and root as you do cuttings.

By division

Plants that make clumps or multiple crowns—African violets, clivias, some orchids, and some ferns—can be propagated by division. Pull a plant apart so that each section has a bit of crown and some root. If plants are massive like the spider-plant or woody, like *Ficus lyrata* sever the growths with a clean, sharp knife, preferably sterilized. Cut off the foliage to encourage new growth; plant the divisions in small pots.

Air layering

Philodendrons, rubber plants, and dieffenbachias—those with woody stems —are often difficult to reproduce from cuttings and are best propagated by air layering. Either remove a strip of bark about 1-inch long directly below a leaf node, or cut a notch in the stem. In either case wrap a big clump of moist moss around the bare wood and cover with a piece of plastic secured top and bottom with string. There must be a moisture-proof seal for growth to start.

Air layering takes time. It may be six to nine months before roots form. When you can see roots in the moss ball, sever the new plant just below the ball of roots. Then pot it.

From seed

Calceolaria, cobea, asparagus-fern, and many other plants are readily increased from seed. Growing from seed is a fascinating and simple way of getting many plants for little money. Sow seeds sparingly and evenly in a propagating mix kept at 70 to 75F; bottom heat hastens germination. Soil heating cables are helpful, or you can set the flat or other container of seeds on top of an electric refrigerator where it is warm.

Begonia and many other seeds are so fine they are like powder. Don't cover these. Sow them as thinly as possible on top of the vermiculite or other medium and press them in place. Mixing them with sand makes even distribution easier. Cover

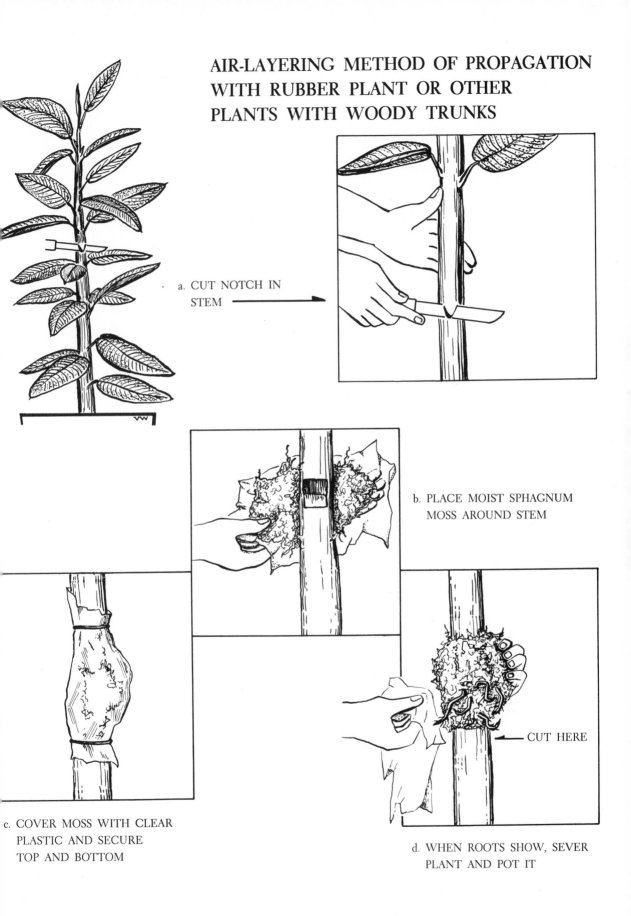

AIR-LAYERING METHOD OF PROPAGATION WITH RUBBER PLANT OR OTHER PLANTS WITH WOODY TRUNKS

a. CUT NOTCH IN STEM

b. PLACE MOIST SPHAGNUM MOSS AROUND STEM

c. COVER MOSS WITH CLEAR PLASTIC AND SECURE TOP AND BOTTOM

CUT HERE

d. WHEN ROOTS SHOW, SEVER PLANT AND POT IT

larger seeds like those of coleus and impatiens to their own depth. Label each planting. Keep the rooting mixture moderately moist; never allow it to get soggy or to dry out. Remove the cover of the container for a few minutes several times a day. Place the seed boxes in the shade until you see signs of growth; then move them to bright light.

As soon as leaves sprout, feed seedlings with diluted plant food. Pot them individually before they get crowded. Then place them in a bright warm spot for a few weeks before moving them to more permanent quarters in the indoor garden.

7

House-Plant Clinic

Good culture and catching trouble before it starts go a long way toward avoiding pest and disease. Keep your plants well groomed; pick off dead leaves and faded flowers. Wipe or mist foliage at least once a week with clear tepid water. This cleansing tends to remove insect eggs and spider mites and, in general, discourages other pests. It also helps to develop a healthy sheen, and is preferable to the use of leaf-shining preparations that clog leaf pores. Plants too large to move easily can be freshened in place by wiping leaves with a damp cloth.

Is it poor culture?

Sometimes the decline of a plant is the result of improper culture. Discolored or falling leaves and premature bud drop are not necessarily caused by insects or disease. Better check culture before you spray or dust. It may be that repotting to improve drainage, a different method of watering, an increase in humidity, or simply fresh air regularly admitted will bring plants back to health.

Unhealthy Conditions and Possible Causes

Symptoms	Probable causes
Brown or yellow leaves	Too high heat, too low humidity, not enough fresh air, soil too dry or too wet.
Yellow or white rings on leaves	Use of cold water especially on African-violets; apply tepid water or let it stand overnight to reach room temperature.
Leaf drop	Temperature extremes, cold water, too low humidity.

61

Pale leaves, weak growth	Too little light; too high heat; too much food, particularly if high in nitrogen.
Slow growth	Sour, poorly-drained soil; cramped roots; or plant may be in a *naturally* somewhat inactive period.
Bud drop	Grown too hot or too cold, shocked by a draught or change from greenhouse to home; most likely too low humidity.
Collapse of plant	Extreme cold or heat, root rot from poor drainage.
Dry crumbling leaves, especially on English ivy	Too high heat, too low humidity (or red spider).

If it's pest or disease

Almost inevitably indoor plants, even with the best of culture, at some time suffer an insect attack, more rarely a disease infection. It is good policy to schedule spraying with an all-purpose preparation once a month, and always before you bring plants in from the garden in fall. My preference for spraying is malathion; furthermore, isolate any plant that looks limp or sickly or isn't growing well. Of course, give strangers a trial period before admitting them to your indoor garden, and do give each plant enough room so that air can circulate around it; crowding is always unhealthy.

If you discover a light insect attack, you might first try to clean it up with a vigorous spray of clear or soapy water, followed by a clear rinse. If the infestation is heavy, better apply a commercial insecticide. Some come in powder form for dusting, others are liquids to be diluted with water for spraying. Avoid strong, outdoor preparations for your indoor garden. Try to select either a good all-purpose material or a specific one, realizing that a miticide won't cure disease and the spray that kills mealy bugs won't clean up scale. Know what you are fighting before you do battle. And alternate preparations since they have different effects and one may emphasize one kind of clean-up, another be more effective for something else.

Dunking an infested plant in a pail of solution is the surest kill. Cover the soil with a piece of foil, invert the plant, and douse it up and down several times. Let it drip-dry out of the sun; then rinse with clear water. More trouble than in-place spraying, dunking in a malathion or other solution, as I do, in the end usually provides the quickest clean-up.

31   Lush foliage plants in a floor-planter bin add grace to this living-room scene. Plants include schefflera at left, ivy in center, and aphelandra at right. Hedrich-Blessing photo

If you have only a few plants, keep on hand an all-purpose aerosol bomb. For a number of plants, these push-button cans tend to be expensive, but they are certainly a convenience. In any case, read the label to be sure of what you are buying. Always spray the whole plant—leaves, stems, and under as well as over the foliage. Don't spray at close range; the recommended distance is 12 to 14 inches away.

Systemics—insecticides to apply to soil—are proving a boon for pot plants. One application will protect most flowering and foliage plants (but not ferns and palms) from the majority of sucking and chewing insects for six to eight weeks. Systemics come in granular form; spread them over the soil and then water the plant thoroughly. From the roots, the insecticide is drawn up into the sap stream, thus making it toxic.

Whatever products you select, be sure to follow the manufacturer's directions. When most plants are grown under good cultural conditions with the monthly all-purpose spray, there is little likelihood of trouble. (African-violets are more vulnerable than most and their special problems are discussed under *Saintpaulia* in the Dictionary.) I list these various difficulties below just in case. What is most important is not to grow plants too warm—always an invitation to red spider especially on English ivy—and to assure some daily fresh air, indirectly, of course, in very cold weather. A hot, close atmosphere can spell disaster.

32　Three undemanding house plants. *Cryptanthus zonatus*, *Peperomia*, and *Bromelia*. U.S.D.A. photo

Diagnosis and Treatment

CONDITION	CAUSE	CONTROL
White cottony clusters in stem and leaf axils; undersized foliage; spindly growth	Mealy bugs	Spray with malathion or apply a systemic to soil or remove just a few bugs with an alcohol-dipped Q-tip. Discard if heavily infested.
Leaves deformed, streaked or silvery with dark specks	Thrips, almost invisible yellow, brown, or black sucking insects	Spray with malathion.
Green, black, red, or pink insects especially on new growth; sticky, shiny leaves, often cupped; sooty mold; plants stunted	Aphids	Spray with malathion, nicotine, or lindane, or apply a systemic to soil.
Plants stunted, crowns bunched, leaves cupped up or down, buds blackened	Cyclamen or broad mite, especially on African-violets	Spray with Dimite or Kalthane every 2 to 4 weeks as preventive; use sterilized soil.
Fine webs at leaf and stem axils and underneath; leaves mottled turning gray or brown and crumbly	Microscopic red spider mites	Try vigorous water spray above and below to break webs or spray with Dimite or Aramite.
Swarming "moths," sooty deposits, leaves stippled or yellowing	White flies	Spray with malathion.
Clusters of little brown or gray or white lumps, plant losing vigor	Scale; insects with hard or soft shells (not to be confused with seed cases on underside of fern fronds)	Pick off, if a few, or scrub with strong soapy solution; or spray with malathion or nicotine.

Holes in leaves	Slugs or snails	Apply Bug-Getta around and near pot.
Leaves gray or watery, green or yellow; crown rotting	Bacterial blight	Spray with Captan or Fermate.
Flowers, leaves, and stalks spotted or circled	Virus disease	Best to destroy plant through spraying every 3 days with Zineb *may* check this.
Leaves coated white	Mildew	Spray with Karathane or Phaltan, or dust with Zineb or sulfur.
Gray mold on flowers and leaves	Botrytis blight	Get rid of badly infected plant; or try spraying with Ferbam or Zineb; cut out diseased sections; water less; avoid crowding.
Swelling on leaves and corky ridges	Edema (particularly ivy geraniums)	Water less, especially on dark or humid days.

Home remedies

For years I have used various home remedies for ailing plants, and I still resort to these before reaching for an insecticide.

A thorough washing or strong spraying at the sink often eliminates aphids. A solution of a tablespoon of alcohol to a quart of soapy water applied with a small brush will do the job, too. Dip small plants (soil covered with foil); hand-wash medium-sized ones, and spray large specimens. A mixture of soap and water sprayed on ailing plants will deter red spider, and mealy bugs can often be eradicated with a solution of equal parts water and alcohol, followed by a washing with soap and water and a rinsing with clear water. Or go over an infested plant with a Q-tip dipped in alcohol. Gently scrub off scale with a stiff brush dipped in soap water.

Potatoes cut in half and laid on the soil will lure snails and sow bugs to the surface where you can destroy them. Hot water (90F) poured over soil of a plant will chase springtails into a saucer from which you can wash them away.

To increase humidity for a sickly plant losing leaves, draw over it a plastic bag, perforated in a few places. Secure the bag around the pot rim with a rubber band.

66

Improved health is often evident in a week or so; leaves stop falling, and buds begin to form and open. The bag can be removed for days at a time if the plant is to go on display. Brunfelsia, gardenia, and ailing ferns have responded to the bag treatment.

Soil ailments

Soil for plants must be friable and porous but after repeated watering and feeding, soils may build up an accumulation of chemical salts. These salts must be flushed from the soil or else they become locked in and set up a roadblock so roots cannot get nutrients. Put plants under a strong stream of water—several times—to wash out accumulated salts.

Soils that contain a large portion of organic matter—leaf mold, peatmoss, or humus—are more apt to become sour as a result of repeated waterings. Charcoal granules help to aerate the soil and prevent this condition.

Occasionally, the surface of moist humusy soil will harbor springtails, minute insects. They can damage tender seedlings but can be eradicated by spraying the surface of the soil with malathion.

Root nematodes are tiny eelworms that suck juice from roots and leaves and cause knots or swellings on the roots. Although there are nematocides to kill young nematodes (VC-13 is one), these chemicals are extremely poisonous and best not used at home. I find it better to discard an infested plant.

Edema (oedema) is a condition that occurs when plants rapidly absorb water but moisture loss from leaves is slow; extra moisture backs up and cells burst. Leaves develop water-soaked spots that get reddish brown. On cloudy days when soil is warm and moist and air is cool and moist, edema gets started, Avoid overwatering plants especially in cloudy damp weather; raise heat, lower humidity, and space out plants; don't mist foliage. Allow soil to get quite dry before watering. Generally, plants will recover from edema—but not quickly.

33   *Acalypha wilkesiana*. Merry Gardens photo

8

Dictionary of 1000 House Plants

In so far as possible *Hortus Second* by L. H. and E. Z. Bailey has been followed for botanical nomenclature, *Exotica* by A. B. Graf for common names. Hyphenation is in accordance with the recommendations of the Committee on Nomenclature of the Garden Writers Association of America. An asterisk preceding a name indicates that the plant is a miniature.

ABUTILON **flowering-maple**
Malvaceae **45-55F**

Vigorous free-flowering shrubs to 36 inches with large bell-shaped, paper-thin flowers of orange, yellow, red, or white—a colorful display from May to August. The maple foliage is handsome, green or variegated. Grow in pots or hanging baskets. Give full sun, moderate fertilizing, and buckets of water. Plants tend to get leggy, so pinch young shoots to get bushy growth. Keep potbound to promote bloom. Start new ones from cuttings or seed in spring.

A. *hybridum*—spotted leaves, flowers of various colors:
'Apricot', orange blooms
'Golden Fleece', yellow blooms
'Souvenir de Bonn', orange-and-red flowers
A. *megapotamicum variegatum*—green-and-yellow leaves, red-and-yellow flowers

A. *striatum*—orange flowers
thompsonii—variegated leaves, yellow flowers

ACALYPHA **chenille-plant**
Euphorbiaceae **65-75F**

Showy strings of red or greenish-white flowers spring from leaf axils throughout the year. Green or copper-colored foliage. Provide a sunny window and keep soil evenly moist with humidity around 50 per cent. Feed while plants are growing. For a good show, put several plants in one container. Propagate by cuttings in fall.

A. *godseffiana*—to 20 inches, bright green, yellow-edged leaves; green-white flowers.
A. *hispida*—to 30 inches, hairy green leaves, bright red blooms.
A. *wilkesiana macrophylla*—to 30 inches, bronze-and-copper foliage, red blooms.
macafeana—to 30 inches, coppery leaves, grown for foliage.

69

ACANTHUS   Grecian-urn-plant
Acanthaceae   50-70F

Decorative plants to 36 inches that make effective accents and require little attention. Leaves are ornamental, lush, and green; the showy summer flowers, white, lilac, or rose. Give bright light and keep soil wet during growth; 30 to 50 per cent humidity. Let die down after flowering with soil barely moist. Propagate by seeds or by division of rhizomes in early spring. Excellent for patio tubs.

A. *mollis*—broad glossy green leaves, thrusting heads of pink-and-white flowers, best.
A. *montanus*—narrow dark green leaves with spines, pink blooms.

ACHIMENES   rainbow-flower
Gesneriaceae   60-70F

These offer about the best possible summer display. With glossy cut-leaf foliage and flowers in all colors of the rainbow except green, they are indispensable for window gardens, sunny terraces, or in baskets hung from pergolas. Some are compact to 16 inches, others upright from 16 to 20 inches, and many are basket plants with 20-inch flowering cascades. Start 6 to 8 tubers in an 8-inch bulb pan anytime from January on. When growth is a few inches high, give each plant a 5-inch pot. Bloom appears in 6 to 8 weeks and continues for 4 months in sun. Do provide one special requirement: Keep soil evenly moist; if it dries while plants are in growth or bloom, they may go dormant. When flowers fade, store pots indoors in a dim cool place. In early spring, repot the tubers in fresh soil in the same pots. Tubers multiply quickly or grow from seeds.

A. *antiirrhina*—upright to 20 inches, scarlet-and-yellow flowers.
A. 'Charm'—compact to 16 inches, pink blooms.
A. *flava*—basket plant with golden yellow blooms.
A. 'Francois Cardinaux'—to 20 inches, lavender-and-white flowers.
A. *grandiflora*—to 26 inches, purple flowers with white throats.
A. 'Master Ingram'—to 20 inches, orange-and-red blooms.

A. 'Purple King'—to 16 inches, popular, floriferous.
A. *pedunculata*—to 28 inches with fiery orange flowers.
A. 'Purity'—to 16 inches, lovely soft white.
A. 'Vivid'—to 18 inches, dazzling basket plant with orange-and-magenta bloom.

ACINETA
Orchidaceae   55-75F

Splendid epiphytic orchids that bear a profusion of yellow red-spotted flowers on 24-inch pendent stems; leaves are broad, a pleasing green. Give morning sun and pot in large-grade fir bark in slatted redwood baskets; keep fir bark moist but never wet. Mist foliage frequently after leaves mature. Flower spikes develop at the base of the bulbs; don't let water lodge in young buds or they will rot. New plants from specialists.

A. *densa*—2-inch flowers in spring.
A. *superba*—larger flowers, to 3 inches, in summer.

ACORUS   miniature flagplant
Araceae   40-50F

Tufted little plants to about 10 inches with irislike leaves, attractive but hardly showy, for a north window. I have never seen them bloom indoors; generally they are used as base plantings for specimen plants like dracaena or podocarpus. Keep soil moist; these are marsh-growers. For more plants, divide clumps in spring or fall. Favorites of the Chinese and Japanese who use them for bonsai.

A. *gramineus pusillus*—flat waxy dark green leaves.
   variegatus—green-and-white leathery leaves.

ADIANTUM   maidenhair fern
Polypodiaceae   55-70F

Delicate lacy fronds and wiry black stems make these fast-growing, decorative ferns desirable even if they do need a little pampering. Mainly, protect them from strong sun in summer and excessive heat. Keep soil evenly moist and provide 40 to 60 per cent humidity. Syringe foliage at least once a week and occasionally stand

34 *Acorus gramineus variegatus.* Merry Gardens photo

plants in a pail of water until all roots are moistened. Frond tips are delicate and if they drag on sills, they turn brown. If possible, place pots on pedestals (inverted pots will do) or grow in baskets. Propagate by division of clumps.

A. *bellum*—to 12 inches, fluffy fronds; easier to grow than most.
A. *cuneatum*—to 20 inches, most popular, elegant and graceful.
A. *hispidulum*—to 12 inches, forked leaves.
A. *tenerum Wrightii*—to 20 inches, pale pink-green fronds maturing to lush deep green.

ADROMISCHUS
Crassulaceae 60-75F

Miniature plants from Cape Province in South Africa with thick, beautifully formed and colored leaves; they rarely bloom indoors. Easy to grow in a sunny window. Keep soil somewhat dry; these are desert plants. Propagation from offsets.

* A. *clavifolius*—to 6 inches with clusters of fat club-shaped silver-green leaves.

* A. *cooperi*—to 12 inches, small leaves dotted red.
* A. *cristatus*—to 10 inches, thick crested leaves and red stems.
* A. *maculatus*—to 10 inches, thick, chocolate-brown foliage.

AECHMEA   living-vase-plant
Bromeliaceae 60-75F

Almost carefree, these small, medium, and large plants are usually vase-shaped with brilliantly colored leaves—variegated, deep red, some appearing lacquered. The flower spike is usually long, the small flowers hidden in the bracts. Many bear white, red, or blue berries that last for several months. Give bright light, and pot in fir bark or osmunda; do not fertilize. Keep the "vase" filled with water. Most species bloom in spring or summer, a few in winter. When flowers fade, suckers appear at the base of plants. Cut them off when they are 2 to 4 inches high and pot separately.

A. *calyculata*—to 20 inches, crown of vivid yellow in April.

71

A. *fasciata*—to 24 inches, tufted blue-and-pink flower-heads in spring.

A. 'Maginali'—to 30 inches, outstanding hybrid with pendent red flowers, usually in winter, followed by blue-black berries.

A. *pubescens*—12 to 20 inches, wheat-colored blooms in fall followed by white berries.

A. *racinae*—to 14 inches, red, black, and yello.√ flowers at Christmas time.

A. *ramosa*—to 40 inches, pyramidal head of yellow flowers with red bracts in summer.

A. *weilbachii*—to 20 inches, lavendar flowers with red bracts, usually in winter.

AEONIUM

Crassulaceae 55-70F

Striking plants from 10 to 36 inches across; some rosettes hug the soil, others perch on stem-ends. Give bright light rather than sun and keep plants in growth almost dry. In winter, give only enough water for leaves to stay firm. Add sand to the basic house-plant mix. Spring and summer blooming. Plants die after flowering but offshoots are usually produced first.

A. *arboreum*—to 36 inches, thick stem topped with rosette of green leaves, yellow flowers.

atropurpureum—to 36 inches, coppery-red leaves, golden-yellow flowers.

A. *decorum*—to 30 inches, coppery-red leaves and white flowers.

A. *domesticum*—to 20 inches, shrubby with hairy foliage, yellow flowers.

A. *haworthii*—to 18 inches, blue-green leaves edged red, pale yellow blooms.

A. *nobile*—to 24 inches, olive-green leaves, scarlet blooms.

A. *tabulaeforme*—to 20 inches, my favorite, an open rosette of small fresh green leaves, yellow flowers.

AERIDES

Orchidaceae 55-75F

These lovely free-flowering epiphytic orchids are valued for their pretty flowers and sweet fragrance. Most species have dark green leathery strap leaves. Waxy flowers lasting three weeks are borne in pendent racemes, sometimes 20 inches long. The dominant color is pale pink, although white also occurs. Place at your sunniest window and pot in medium-grade fir bark. Mist frequently and give ample moisture all year; 40 to 60 per cent humidity. Mostly summer-flowering. Buy seedlings from specialists.

A. *affine*—to 20 inches, dark rose flowers with purple spots.

A. *crassifolium*—to 14 inches, amethyst-purple blooms, generally spotted.

A. *falcatum*—to 14 inches, white and rose, usually spotted.

A. *maculosum*—to 20 inches, light rose with purple spots.

A. *odoratum*—to 24 inches, popular, with large fragrant white flowers stained magenta.

AESCHYNANTHUS
(Trichosporum)   lipstick-vine

Gesneriaceae 60-75F

Summer-flowering, these are not the easiest plants to bring into bloom but they are well worth the effort. They are trailing epiphytes to 3 feet with dark glossy leaves and a wealth of tubular orange or red flowers. Don't make the mistake of keeping them in hot sun; they prefer a somewhat shaded position. In active growth they require plenty of water. Give plants warmth and spray frequently to try to keep humidity high, between 50 and 70 per cent. Propagate by layering or from cuttings.

A. *lobbianus*—clusters of brilliant red flowers at the tips of branches.

A. *longiflorus*—robust, masses of red blooms.

A. *marmoratus*—tubular green flowers with brown spots.

A. *pulcher*—red-and-yellow flowers.

A. *speciosus*—spectacular orange-red blooms.

AFRICAN-VIOLET, see SAINTPAULIA and GESNERIADS

AGAPANTHUS   lily-of-the-Nile

Liliaceae 50-70F

Handsome large or dwarf tub plants with fleshy green leaves and erect April and May spikes crowned with great spheres of white or dazzling blue blooms. Give a bright window and keep plants potbound. Water freely until after flowering, then carry somewhat dry through late summer. In winter, foliage dies down naturally and plants can be stored in basement or garage at 40 to 50F with watering about once a month. Try dwarfs indoors; others for a patio. Best to grow on undisturbed in same container for several years. Propagate by seeds or division of roots when repotting in spring.

A. *africanus*—to 36 inches, the most popular, large umbels of blue flowers.
A. *inapertus*—to 18 inches, compact heads of deep blue.
A. *orientalis*—to 48 inches, blue flowers.
A. 'Dwarf White'—to 24 inches, white blooms.
A. 'Peter Pan'—to 12 inches, dark blue flowers.

AGAVE century-plant
Amaryllidaceae 55-75F

Ten-inch to 5-foot rosettes with stiff succulent leaves in shades of blue, gray, green, banded-white or yellow. Don't expect flowers from plants indoors. Slow-growing, agaves adjust to almost any condition. Provide sandy soil, water once a week, and let grow in the same pot for years. The very large plants are landscape specimens requiring much space; smaller types are bold and dramatic pot plants for porch or window. New ones from offshoots.

A. *americana marginata*—trunkless, to 5 feet, green leaves edged yellow; despite the name, "century-plant," these do not require a century to bloom but flower from 10 years on.
A. *attenuata*—trunk to 3 feet, soft gray-green rosettes.
A. *medio-picta*—trunkless, to 5 feet, yellow center stripes on green leaves.
A. *miradorensis*—trunkless, to 3 feet, the "dwarf century-plant."
A. *victoriae-reginae*—trunkless, a 10-inch rosette of narrow olive-green leaves penciled white—a compact globe of beauty.

AGLAONEMA Chinese-evergreen
Araceae 60-75F

Tough to beat, these plants from tropical forests thrive under untoward conditions. Most species have dark green leaves, some marked with silver or white. Flowers are white. Give bright light or semishade and constant moisture at the roots, or grow in a vase of water. Easy to propagate: cut stems into 3-inch pieces, place in moist sand, and barely cover. Only potbound plants will bloom but bloom they do luxuriantly in late summer and early fall.

A. *commutatum*—to 2 feet, silver markings on dark green leaves.
A. *modestum*—to 2 feet, most popular, waxy dark green foliage.
* A. *pictum*—dwarf to 1-foot, dark green velvety leaves, silver spotted.
A. 'Pseudo-bracteatum'—to 2 feet, generally classed as a hybrid, green foliage splashed yellow.
A. *robelinii*—to 3 feet, blue-green leaves, very robust.
A. *simplex*—to 3 feet, the "Chinese-evergreen," grows like a weed in a jar of water.
A. *treubii*—to 2 feet, lance-shaped blue-green foliage marked with silver.

ALBUCA
Liliaceae 45-60F

South African bulbous plants to 4 feet with basal leaves and erect racemes of flowers, resembling scillas, in spring and summer. Pot 4 bulbs close together in a 6-inch pot for a good display. Provide a sandy soil, full sun, and plenty of water in spring, moderate moisture in summer. After plants bloom, let foliage ripen; then store pots dry in a shady place until fall. Propagate by offsets from mature bulbs.

A. *crinifolia*—to 36 inches, 2-inch white waxy flowers with green midrib.
A. *major*—to 34 inches, lovely pale yellow flowers.
A. *nelsoni*—to 42 inches, white species.

Algerian ivy see HEDERA

ALLAMANDA
Apocynaceae 55-65F

Mostly evergreen climbers with tubular green leaves and waxen flowers in spring and summer. Give full sun and plenty of water during growth. Assure 30 to 50 per cent humidity. In winter, keep soil barely moist. Prune back in spring to keep in bounds; propagate from cuttings. Large species for sun porch, small ones for window gardens.

A. *cathartica hendersonii*—giant to 7 feet, golden yellow flowers.

A. *nerilfolia*—shrub to 3 feet, golden yellow blooms.

A. *violacea*—to 4 feet, climber with startling red-purple flowers.

ALLIUM   flowering onion
Liliaceae 50-70F

Handsome bulbous plants with green strap leaves and lovely umbels of rose, lilac, or white flowers. These onions offer a great deal for little care and bloom well indoors. Pot in sandy soil and grow at a bright window; give plenty of water. Propagate by offsets. Dramatic as cut flowers, they last for days in a vase of water. When they finally fade, spray them with gold or silver paint (from the florist) for a unique decoration.

A. *neapolitanum*—to 30 inches, slender leaves, large starry white flowers.

A. *schoenoprasum*—to 30 inches, round heads of rose-purple blooms.

A. *triquetrum*—to 18 inches, large white flowers.

ALLOPHYTON   Mexican-foxglove
Scrophulariaceae 50-70F

A charming little 10-inch plant with long leathery dark green leaves and fragrant tubular lavendar flowers in spring and summer. Place in a sunny window and keep soil evenly moist. Stubborn to make bloom. Propagate by seeds in spring.

A. *mexicanum*

ALOCASIA
Araceae 65-75F

Dramatic exotics with showy velvety-green foliage veined copper or gray, silver or red. The heart-shaped leaves are held high on thin stems. From tropical Asia, these plants prefer a shaded location. Add peatmoss to the recommended soil mixture and keep this moist; feed monthly with diluted fertilizer; make sure of perfect drainage. Although these require care and higher humidity—to 80 per cent—than most indoor subjects, a well-grown specimen is a beautiful sight and worth growing. Propagate from suckers.

A. *amazonica*—to 20 inches, bushy with white-veined scalloped leaves.

A. *chantrieri*—to 20 inches, bushy, handsome with dark green leaves and gray veins.

A. *cuprea*—to 15 inches, compact, shiny purple-green foliage.

A. *lowii grandis*—to 24 inches, metallic brown-green foliage.

veitchii—to 24 inches, smaller marbled arrow leaves, brownish green.

A. *watsoniana*—to 28 inches, "queen of alocasias," with silver veins on corrugated blue-green leaves.

A. *zebrina*—to 18 inches, green leaves with brown zebra bands.

ALOE
Liliaceae 55-75F

Succulents grown for their handsome rosettes of all-green or spotted leaves. Although they have soft pulpy foliage, they are often confused with the agaves that have tough fibrous leaves. Plants are divided into three groups: small, for windows and dish gardens; medium growers for plant rooms; giants for tubs outdoors. Give sun and a sandy well-drained soil. Keep barely moist; a saturated condition is fatal. Spectacular fall or winter, orange, or red, or yellow tubular blooms, but rarely indoors. New plants from offshoots.

A. *arborescens*—to 10 feet, the "candelabra aloe," with thick blue-green leaves.

* A. *aristata*—6 inches across, the "lace aloe"; green-gray rosette dotted white and tipped with white marginal teeth.

* A. *brevifolia*—3- to 4-inch gray-green rosette; occasionally bears a tall spike of red flowers for me in late fall.

* A. *ciliaris*—6-inch, soft, green-white toothed leaves with sprawling growth and pencil stems.

* A. *globosa*—4 to 7 inches, the "crocodile aloe," with gray-green leaves.

A. *nobilis*—to about 2 feet, the "gold-spined aloe," with bright green leaves edged yellow.

A. *variegata*—to 12 inches, the "partridge-breast aloe"; with rosette of three-cornered, dark rich green leaves marbled and margined white.

35 *Aloe.* Merry Gardens photo

ALPINIA ginger
                        Zingiberaceae 50-70F

Good ornamental plants to 36 inches from the South Seas and New Guinea. They need shade from summer sun and ample moisture; 50 per cent humidity. Propagate by division of clumps.

A. *purpurata*—to 36 inches with dense clusters of red bracts coming from the center of the leafy stem.
A. *sanderae*—to 16 inches, pale green leaves edged white; grown for foliage.

ALTERNANTHERA
                        Amaranthaceae 55-75F

Small decorative foliage plants with pretty diminutive white flowers. Grow at a south window, keep soil on the dry side, and provide 50 per cent humidity. Charming for a window sill. Propagate from cuttings.

* A. *ramosissima*—8 to 12 inches, broad-pointed metallic wine-red leaves.
* A. *versicolor*—to 3 inches with copper or red leaves.

Aluminum-plant see PILEA

Amaryllis see HIPPEASTRUM

Amazon-lily see EUCHARIS

ANANAS pineapple
                        Bromeliaceae 50-70F

Spiny-leaved plants with handsome foliage, usually striped green, cream, and pink but, in some species, it is plain green. Pink, red and white bracts on tall spikes are dramatic and appear in summer. Give sandy soil, bright light, and moderate moisture. Large species are excellent as tub plants; smaller ones for pot growing.

75

Wipe leaves with damp cloth to bring out their beauty. New plants from offsets.

A. *comosus*—30- to 36-inch rosette, the pineapple of commerce, dark green leaves.

   variegatus—36-inch rosette, spectacular yellow-green-pink foliage.

A. *nanus*—to 15 inches, fresh green leaves, available in fruit at florist shops.

Angel-lily see CRINUM

Angel's-trumpet see DATURA

ANGRAECUM   comet orchid
Orchidaceae 55-75F

Amenable large and small epiphytes with white flowers and leathery leaves. The blossoms have a long spur, sometimes to 12 inches. Not demanding as to temperature or humidity, plants thrive with little care. Pot in large-grade fir bark, place in a bright spot, and keep mix moderately moist. Propagation by offshoots.

* A. *compactum*—to 3 inches, with 4-inch flowers in winter.
A. *eburneum*—to 36 inches, with alternating rows of white bloom in late fall or early winter.
* A. *falcatum*—to 6 inches, fragrant white flowers in late fall or early winter.
A. *veitchii*—to 24 inches, star-shaped blooms from January on.

ANSELLIA   spider orchid
Orchidaceae 50-70F

You cannot find a better orchid than this. Free-flowering and easy-to-grow, this epiphyte is cane-type with crowns of bright green leaves. Thriving specimens to 4 feet bear up to a hundred red-and-yellow flowers on branching stems. Grow in sun with plenty of water. Pot in large-grade fir bark and maintain 40 to 60 per cent humidity. You can get more plants (and young ones do bloom) by division. A. *africanus* is also sold as A. *gigantea* and A. *nilotica*. All have the typical red-and-yellow flowers. Best to buy mature plants.

A. *africanus*

ANTHURIUM   flamingo-flower
Araceae 65-80F

From Central and South American jungles, these plants of striking foliage and winter and spring "lacquered" flowers make superb indoor decoration. They need a potting mix of half standard soil and half fine-grade fir bark to insure perfect drainage. Grow in a shaded location and keep soil moist. Unless you can give warmth with 80 per cent humidity, better not try them. They require time and patience but are worth every effort. More plants from seeds.

A. *andraeanum*—to 16 inches, green foliage; red, white, coral, or pink flowers.
A. *bakeri*—to 15 inches, brilliant red blooms.
A. *crystallinum*—to 14 inches, perhaps the most handsome with velvety green leaves, silver veined, flowers insignificant.
A. *forgetti*—to 16 inches, similar to the above but with oval leaves.
A. *scandens*—climbing, to 36 inches, dark green foliage.
A. *scherzerianum*—to 16 inches, most familiar, red flowers, favorites for arrangements.
A. *warocqueanum*—30-inch rosette, long velvety leaves with pale green veins; outstanding.

APHELANDRA
Acanthaceae 55-75F

Long-lasting terminal clusters of orange or yellow spring or summer flowers with gray-green or dark green leaves attractively veined white. Supply a rich porous soil and rather small pots in view of the size of the plants. They grow rapidly in sun and need plenty of water while active; less at other times. They tend to get leggy in winter so best start new ones annually from cuttings.

A. *aurantiaca roezlii*—to 16 inches, vivid orange-red blooms.
A. *chamissoniana*—to 14 inches, the "zebra-plant" popular, with cheerful yellow bracts.
A. *squarrosa louisae*—compact, to 20 inches, shiny corrugated leaves, shaded yellow bracts.

Apostle-plant see NEOMARICA

Arabian coffeeplant see COFFEA

36 (Above) *Anthurium scherzerianum hybrid*; Merry Gardens photo; (below) Left, *Anthurium andreanum*, right, A. *crystallinum*. U.S.D.A. photo

Arabian jasmine see JASMINUM

Aralia see DIZYGOTHECA

ARAUCARIA   Norfolk-Island-pine
Araucariacea   50-70F

This green-needled 20- to 48-inch plant looks like a miniature Christmas tree. It is easily grown in north or bright light and requires only evenly moist soil and deep watering in a pail once a week. An elegant evergreen, it will be with you for years; slow-growing and best kept pot-bound. New plants from seed or by air layering.

A. excelsa

ARDISIA   coralberry
Myrsinaceae   50-60F

A colorful fruit plant for Christmas and often available at supermarkets then. The leaves on this appealing little tree look like holly. The fragrant white flowers are followed by coral-red or white berries that often persist along with a cloud of new bloom. Plants need light and sand added to the standard potting mixture. Keep soil just moist; occasionally give plants a deep soaking in a pail of water and mist foliage frequently; watch out for scale. Propagate by cuttings or seeds.

A. crenata (crispa)—to 30 inches, glossy green leaves and red berries from December through June.

37   *Araucaria excelsa.* Merry Gardens photo

A. *japonica*—to 18 inches, not so colorful but still nice with white berries.

ARIOCARPUS   living-rock cactus
Cactaceae 55-75F

Almost spineless globular desert species with leaflike "foliage" arranged in a spiral, the larger part of the plant below the ground. Lovely large pink or white or lavender flowers crown the top of the plant in summer. Grow in sandy soil in sun with scant watering. Keep in 3- or 4-inch pots, or use in dish gardens. Propagate by offsets.

A. *furfuraceus* (*retusus*)—"seven stars," to 8 inches, pink blooms.
A. *mcdowellii*—to 8 inches, lavender flower.

ARISTOLOCHIA   calico-flower
Aristolochiaceae 55-75F

An unusual vine to 15 feet with flamboyant spotted flowers; leaves heart-shaped, large and light green. Grows rapidly in spring and summer and needs plenty of room. Flowers form on hanging shoots so don't cut these off. For tubs on terraces or in sunrooms rather than for windows. Give full sun and copious watering. Flowers are more curious than pretty. Let rest with little water, but not entirely dry, in winter. New plants from seed.

A. *elegans*—slender woody climber with yellow-green-and-brown flowers.
A. *grandiflora*—yellow-green blooms, veined and spotted purple, with spurs.

Arrowhead see SYNGONIUM

ARTHROPODIUM
Liliaceae 50-70F

This grows to 36 inches with light green grassy leaves and clusters of starry white flowers in February and March. Give sun and plenty of water during active growth and bloom. Decrease moisture after flowering but never let soil dry out completely. Propagate by division.

A. *cirrhatum*

Artillery plant see PILEA

ASCOCENTRUM   carnival orchid
Orchidaceae 55-75F

Their gay colors—orange, red, cerise—have earned these small epiphytes the common name. A well-grown plant bears about forty 1-inch blooms in early spring. The strap foliage is leathery. Plant in medium-grade fir bark in 5-inch pots. Give full sun and copious watering during growth, not so much otherwise; 50 per cent humidity. Charmers for the window. New plants from specialists.

A. *ampullaceum*—to 20 inches, dainty cerise flowers.
A. *curvifolium*—to 14 inches, red blooms.
* A. *miniatum*—to 10 inches, orange flowers.

ASPARAGUS   asparagus-fern
Liliaceae 55-75F

These vining or fountain plants, depending on training, are desirable wherever there is space for them. Some species reach 6 feet, a mass of lovely feathery foliage with tiny whitish-pink fragrant flowers followed by red or purple berries. A specimen is attractive throughout the year, and best of all, easily grown even in north light. Give plenty of water and about once a month, a bucket soaking. Handsome for baskets or set on a pedestal or table. Divide clumps or sow seeds.

A. *asparagoides*—to 36 inches, feathery and ferny; used by florists in arrangements.
A. *plumosus*—to 36 inches, horizontal needle growth.
A. *sprengeri*—"emerald-feather" to 5 feet, an exceptionally good house plant, light green needle foliage.

ASPIDISTRA   cast-iron-plant
Liliaceae 50-70F

These old favorites with long dark green leaves survive almost any situation. The 24-inch foliage is sometimes complimented by sprays of purple-brown flowers. Fine green accents for orphan north windows. Keep soil evenly moist. Grow several plants to a pot for a good display. Split crowns carefully for new plants.

A. *elatior*—shiny green-black leaves.
   variegata—green-and-white striped foliage.

ASPLENIUM   bird's-nest fern
Polypodiaceae   50-70F

Handsome 14- to 30-inch ferns that add interest to the indoor garden with their fresh shiny green fronds, parchment-thin, clustering around a center. Add chopped osmunda to the standard soil mixture. Grow in full light and keep soil evenly moist; provide 50 per cent humidity. Mist often and watch out for scale. Propagate by offsets or spores.

A. *bulbiferum*—the "mother fern" with wiry divided fronds and black stems; plantlets grow on the surface of the leaves and can be separately potted.
A. *nidus*—the "bird's-nest fern," wavy light green fronds; smooth, broad and handsome.

ASTROPHYTUM   star cactus
Cactaceae   55-75F

This easy-to-grow desert genus includes some fine spineless or almost-spineless star-shaped plants with large reddish yellow-centered flowers in spring. Add sand to the standard mix; give full sun, and keep soil somewhat dry. Propagate by offsets.

* A. *asterias*—1 inch tall, 3 inches across; spineless with an eight-segmented dome.
* A. *capricorne*—10 inches tall, globular with white ribs and papery spines.
* A. *myriostigma*—2 inches tall, the "bishop's-hood cactus" spineless, globe divided into five segments.

AUCUBA   gold-dust-tree
Cornaceae   50-70F

To 5 feet indoors, this Japanese evergreen with striking yellow-spotted leaves bears insignificant flowers but pretty red, white, or yellow berries. Give it a semishaded place and plenty of water. Shape young plants by pruning. Good for sunroom or terrace; only young plants are small enough for windows. New ones from cuttings or seeds.

A. *japonica goldieana*

Australian bracken see PTERIS

Azalea see RHODODENDRON

Baby primrose see PRIMULA

Baby's-tears see HELXINE, Chapter 4

Ball cactus see NOTOCACTUS and CACTUS

Bamboo see BAMBUSA

Bamboo palm see CHAMAEDOREA

BAMBUSA   bamboo
Graminea   50-70F

Feathery and tall, plants thrive for years in the same pot, and a well-grown specimen has exceptional beauty. Easy to grow if given a bright airy location and plenty of water. Divide clumps in spring for new plants.

B. *multiplex* 'Chinese Goddess'—to 6 feet, gold-and-green foliage.
B. *nana*—to 40 inches, 3-inch blue-green leaves, stays small.
B. *phyllostachys aurea*—the "golden bamboo," to 10 feet.

Banana see MUSA

BEGONIA
Begoniaceae   55-75F

Favorites for house decoration with several hundred species and thousands of varieties, few begonias require exacting care; most thrive with little attention. For convenience, they are generally divided into these groups:

B. SEMPERFLORENS. These are called "wax begonias," with the wonderful habit of blooming almost all year. Plants have glossy dark green or mahogany-colored leaves and single or semi-double or double blooms in shades of white to fiery red. Give them tight pots and sun and avoid overwatering. They like to be quite dry; too much water rots them quickly. Prune back tops as plants get leggy. Propagate by cuttings or seeds.

* B. 'Andy'—to 6 inches, grass-green leaves, single rose flowers.
B. 'Apple Blossom'—to 12 inches, pale pink double flowers.
B. 'Ballet'—to 12 inches, bronze leaves, double white flowers.

B. 'Cinderella'—to 12 inches, pink single blossoms tipped red.

B. 'Green Thimbleberry'—pale green leaves and crested double pink blooms.

B. 'Jack Horner'—to 12 inches, dark green leaves, pink double flowers.

* B. 'Little Gem'—to 6 inches, bronze leaves, double pink flowers.

B. 'Lucy Locket'—to 10 inches, double pink flowers.

B. 'South Pacific'—to 10 inches, bright orange-red double flowers.

RHIZOMATOUS—These are so-called because of their gnarled and thickened root systems. Leaves are round or star-shaped, in plain or fancy patterns, their textures satiny or nubby. Roots naturally skim the surface of the soil and should not be buried. Rhizomes are food storehouses so these begonias can endure drought when necessary. Tall stalks of flowers appear in early spring or late winter. Provide shallow pots and let soil dry out thoroughly between waterings. Some varieties take a short rest in late winter; water sparingly through these weeks until you see signs of new growth. Propagate by cuttings or seeds.

* B. boweri—to 14 inches, the "eyelash begonia," with delicate green leaves stitched black, pink flowers.

* B. 'China Doll'—to 8 inches, light-green-to-purple leaves, pink blooms.

B. crestabruchii—to 16 inches, the "lettuce leaf begonia," heavily ruffled yellow-green leaves with twisted edges, pink flowers.

B. erythrophylla (feastii)—to 14 inches, the "beefsteak begonia," with crested round green leaves, red underneath, long-stemmed pink flowers.

B. heracleifolia—to 14 inches, the "star begonia," star-shaped leaves, pink blooms.

* B. hydrocotylifolia—to 10 inches, the "pennywort begonia" with round dark green leaves, pink flowers.

B. imperialis 'Otto Forster'—to 14 inches, dark green leaves and white flowers.

B. 'Maphil' ('Cleopatra')—to 20 inches, star-shaped leaves splashed with gold, brown, and chartreuse; tall spikes of pink flowers.

B. ricinifolia—to 16 inches, resembles the castor-bean plant with large green leaves and pink flowers.

B. strigilosa—to 16 inches, brown-spotted green leaves on graceful stems, blush-white flowers.

ANGEL WING. This group is named for its wing-shaped leaves; the roots are fibrous. Provide a constantly moist soil and morning or afternoon sun. Cascades of colorful flowers are the reward. Prune frequently to keep growth in bounds; plants can grow inconveniently tall. Propagate by cuttings.

B. 'Alzasco'—to 36 inches, dark green leaves with silver spots, red blooms in pendent clusters.

B. coccinea—to 48 inches, bright green shiny leaves, coral-red flowers, constant bloom.

B. 'Elvira Swisher'—to 48 inches, large lobed leaves laced with silver, pink blooms.

B. 'Grey Feather'—to 48 inches, shiny arrow leaves, white flowers.

B. maculata—to 40 inches, silver-marked foliage, pink flowers.

B. 'Orange-Rubra'—to 36 inches, clear green leaves sometimes spotted with silver, orange flowers.

B. 'Pink-Rubra'—to 60 inches, bright green pointed leaves, large pink blooms.

B. 'Rubaiyat'—to 48 inches, smooth green foliage, salmon-pink blooms.

B. 'Velma'—to 40 inches, green cupped leaves, red flowers.

HIRSUTE OR HAIRY-LEAVED. These have furry foliage and whiskered flowers, the leaves are round, lobed, or tapered; the blooms, red or pink or white, always impressive. Plants perform superbly even in apartments; they can live with dry air if they must and they can tolerate coolness if they have to. Just be sure they get some winter sun so they will bloom. And a word of caution: Keep them only moderately moist; overwatering causes rot. Propagate by stem cuttings.

B. alleryi—to 30 inches, dark green leaves with white hairs and pale pink flowers.

B. drostii—to 30 inches, very hairy leaves and pink flowers.

B. prunifolia—to 30 inches, cupped leaves and white blooms.

B. scharffiana—to 30 inches, green-red plush leaves, ivory blooms.

B. viaudi—to 36 inches, leaves green on top, red below with fine white hairs; white flowers.

REX. These are mostly rhizomatous, grown for their exquisite patterned leaves. Provide warmth (75F daytime, 65F at night), and high humidity (60 per cent), bright light but not much sun; a north window is fine. Keep soil evenly moist. Most kinds drop their leaves and go dormant in winter; don't try to force them to grow then. Water sparingly and wait for new growth. It will appear about mid-March. Propagate from leaf cuttings or seeds.

B. 'Autumn Glow'—to 14 inches, rose-colored leaves with silver.
B. 'Baby Rainbow'—to 12 inches, cupped silver-green-and-purple leaves.
* *B.* 'Berry's Autumn'—to 8 inches, olive-green leaves with silver spots.
* *B.* 'Calico'—to 8 inches, crimson, green, and silver foliage.
B. 'Cardoza Gardens'—to 16 inches, large purple, silver-and-green foliage, a striking plant.
B. 'Glory of St. Albans'—metallic rose-purple foliage.
B. 'Merry Christmas'—striped with color, mostly red.
B. 'Peace'—metallic red-and-silver leaves.
B. 'Queen of Hanover'—light green leaves banded darker green.
B. 'Red Berry'—wine-red foliage.
B. 'Red Wing'—wine-red leaves with silver edges.
B. 'Thrush'—crimson star-shaped leaves dotted silver.
B. 'Winter Queen'—spiral leaf form, silver, purple, and pink.

TUBEROUS—These are summer-flowering aristocrats of the garden growing to about 24 inches. I have never succeeded with them indoors but I have seen them in bloom under artificial lights. If you are very fond of begonias and want some of these, you can start them indoors for early garden bloom. In March, select large tubers and plant in a 2-inch layer of peatmoss and sand in a flat or similar container. Set the tubers about 2 inches apart and ½ inch deep, hollow-side up. Cover with ¼ inch of the mix. Grow at 60 to 70F and keep barely moist.

When sprouts are 2 inches high, plant tubers in separate 4-inch pots of porous soil. In May, shift to 8- or 9-inch pans or plant directly in the garden.

After frost danger, set your plants outdoors where they will get 3 to 4 hours of sun, and hope for cool weather. Water plants heavily in clear weather, less when it is cloudy. When they are growing well, apply a fertilizer every third week. Let growth continue until leaves turn yellow in fall. Then lift tubers from pots, wash and dry them, and store at 45 to 50F. Keep dry until spring.

B. 'Black Knight'—deep crimson double flowers.
B. 'Flamboyante'—single scarlet.
B. 'Flambeau' — lovely orange-scarlet double flowers.
B. 'Frances Powell'—double pink.
B. 'Mandarin'—salmon-orange double blooms.
B. 'Rosado'—deeply frilled and ruffled pink blooms.
B. 'Sweet Home'—double red.
B. 'Tasso'—semidouble pink.

Hanging-basket begonias are sometimes listed as pendulas or occasionally as Lloydi types by suppliers. With cascading blossoms all summer, they are among the most beautiful of all trailing plants. Give protection from wind and sun; keep soil moderately moist. Plant 2 or 3 medium-sized tubers to a 5-inch pot. Pinch out young shoots early in season to promote growth.
B. 'Andy Lee'—brilliant red. (From Antonelli Bros.)
B. 'Darlene'—pink blossoms with white centers. (From Antonelli Bros.)
B. 'Pink Shower'—clear pink flowers. (From Vetterle and Reinelt.)
B. 'Wild Rose'—dark pink. (From Vetterle and Reinelt.)

B. CHEIMANTHA and *B.* HIEMALIS. These are 20-inch winter-flowering tuberous begonias grown mainly as Christmas and Easter gift plants. Cheimanthas, known as the "Christmas begonia," bloom from November to March. Grow them rather cool and draft-free, the soil constantly wet. When flowers fade, cut back plants severely and grow at 55F until new shoots appear. After the hiemalis type blooms, grow it cool, about 50F, and water sparingly until

V THREE HOLIDAY GIFT PLANTS. (Above left) A showy Christmas cactus for 6 weeks of flowers. (Above right) The bright cyclamen that blooms for 3 months. (Below) A medley of Mikkelsen poinsettias, colorful from Christmas until May. *Park Seed Co. photos*

VI HANDSOME AND EASY TO GROW. A magnificent late summer-blooming orchid, *Rhynchostylis gigantea* from the author's collection. *Joyce Wilson photo*

VII GOOD HOUSE-PLANT ORCHIDS GROWN BY THE AUTHOR. (Upper left) *Cypripedium* hybrid. (Upper right) *Vanda caerulea*, bright with color in November and December. (Lower left) *Dendrobium phalaenopsis. H. Pigors photos* (Lower right) The cinnamon-scented *Lycaste aromatica. Collins photo*

VIII   TENDER BULBS FOR WINDOW GARDENS. (Upper left) Charming
calla lilies in many colors (Upper right) 'Peter Pan', a small version
of the great lily-of-the-Nile, *Agapanthus.* (Lower right) *Scilla Peruvi-
ana* a larger relative of the familiar hardy garden type. (Lower left)
The Aztec-lily, *Sprekelia,* for color and drama. *Brown Bulb Ranch
photos*

spring. Then shake off soil around tuber and repot. Grow at 65F and keep soil moderately wet through summer.

B. cheimantha

'Gloire de Sceaux'—rose-colored.
'Lady Mac'—pink or white.
'Marjorie Gibbs'—pale pink.
'Spirit of Norway'—vibrant red.
'Tove'—rose-colored.

B. hiemalis

'Altrincham Pink'—large long-lasting double pink blooms.
'Emily Clibran'—double pink, considered one of the best.

'John C. Mensing'—free-flowering double orange flowers.

BELOPERONE shrimp-plant
Acanthaceae 55-75F

Most satisfactory flowering plants for a sunny window, with paper-thin bracts and tiny white flowers, deep green leaves. Let these 3- to 4-foot plants dry out between waterings. Prune back leggy growth in late summer. Propagate by cuttings.

B. guttata—most popular, coral-colored bracts.

'Red King'—cascades of red bracts.
'Yellow Queen'—red bracts, yellow blooms.

38   Beloperone guttata 'Yellow Queen'. **Merry Gardens photo**

Bermuda-buttercup see OXALIS

BIFRENARIA

Orchidaceae 55-75F

An uncommonly beautiful genus of 20-inch epiphytic orchids with 10- to 16-inch dark green leaves and impressive colorful flowers in spring. Undemanding, plants bloom readily if they are properly rested. After they flower, keep them almost dry and in a dim place for about 2 months with only an occasional misting, about once a week. Then give bright light and plenty of water through summer. New plants from suppliers.

B. harrisoniae—large waxy white flowers, magenta lip.
B. tyrianthina—lovely pink-and-red flowers on erect stems.

BILLBERGIA living-vase-plant

Bromeliaceae 55-75F

Decorative plants, mostly large, with multicolored foliage and bizarre flowers, perfect for indoor growing. Some have gray-green, some silver-green, others, purple leaves. Flowers are small but the colorful bracts are striking—red or pink or purple. Pot in fir bark or an osmunda-and-soil mix. Give bright light and keep vase filled with water. Good for planters in public places. Propagation by offshoots.

B. amoena—to 16 inches, shiny green leaves, rose bracts in spring or summer.
* *B. morelii*—to 10 inches, green leaves, blue flowers in red sheaths in summer.
B. nutans—to 30 inches, "queen's-tears," chartreuse, pink, and cerise flowers in winter.
B. pyramidalis—to 24 inches, golden-green leaves, orange-pink flowers and bracts in summer.
   'Fantasia'—to 24 inches, robust hybrid with multicolored foliage, red bracts and blue flowers in fall.
B. zebrina—to 40 inches, gray-green foliage flecked with silver, cascading stem of rose bracts, usually in summer.

Bird-of-paradise see STRELITZIA

Bird's-nest fern see ASPLENIUM and FERNS

Bishop's-hood cactus see ASTROPHYTUM

Black-eyed-Susan-vine see THUNBERGIA

BLECHNUM tree fern

Polypodiaceae 55-75F

Seldom seen but made to order for warm dry houses, these tree ferns offer splendid vertical accents. Unlike most ferns, they will grow in low humidity with regular watering and good light. Young leaves are copper and green, maturing to a lovely dark green. Avoid overwatering. Propagate by spores or by offsets.

B. occidentale—to 24 inches, for windows.
B. brasiliense—to 48 inches, for plant room or public places.

Blood-lily see HAEMANTHUS

Blue orchid see VANDA and ORCHIDS

Blue-sage see ERANTHEMUM

Boston fern see NEPHROLEPSIS and FERNS

BOUGAINVILLEA paper-flower

Nyctaginaceae 50-60F

Too often overlooked, these vines offer brilliant color for little effort. Some grow to 20 feet outdoors in temperate climates. Indoors, 2- to 15-foot plants bloom a long time in summer with vivid bracts. Plants need sun and constant moisture in summer; in winter, grow them somewhat dry. Cut them back whenever they get too large. There are some splendid varieties. New plants from seed.

B. 'Barbara Karst'—tall bushy grower with cascading masses of red bracts.
B. glabra—strong vine, purplish-pink bracts.
B. Harrisii—variegated foliage, low bushy growth, white flowers and purple bracts.
B. 'Temple Fire'—low and compact, red to cerise bracts.

Brake fern see PTERIS and FERNS

BRASSAVOLA

Orchidaceae 55-75**F**

Small epiphytes perfect for windows, with large flamboyant white fall flowers, usually scented. Grow in 4- or 5-inch pots of fir bark kept quite dry. Give plenty of sun and good humidity, at least 50 per cent. New plants from specialists.

B. acaulis—to 12 inches, grassy foliage, pure white flowers with heart-shaped lip.
B. cucullata—to 12 inches, similar to above but with greenish flowers.
* *B. nodosa*—to 10 inches, the popular "lady-of-the-night orchid" with sweet-scented white blooms; one plant perfumes an entire room.

Brazilian edelweiss see RECHSTEINERIA

BROMELIA   volcano-plant

Bromeliaceae 55-75**F**

In bloom with fiery centers of red, these large plants are awesome. Leaves are dark green and heavily spined, so wear gloves when handling them. Pot in equal parts of osmunda and soil mix; give sun and even moisture all year. Not demanding about humidity. Good tub plants, suited to public rooms and lobbies. New plants by offshoots; remove them when they have several leaves and pot separately.

B. balansae—24 to 36 inches across, smallest available.
B. humilis—36- to 50-inch rosettes, a beautiful giant.

BROMELIADS

Ten years ago, these plants were rarely seen; today with their colorful bracts and decorative foliage they make any interior a glorious greenery; often known as institutional plants. They are almost carefree and can survive in shade for many months. In the home, too, they scoff at neglect and still furnish color and grace. There are small, medium, and giant species. Most form rosettes of leaves; some, tubular vases of foliage. There are epiphytes and terrestrial kinds; both succeed in a mixture of osmunda and soil. Keep center of plants filled with water, the potting mix barely moist.

Bright sun makes foliage glow with color. The true beauty of bromeliads lies in the bright bracts of spectacular color that is vibrant for six months—cerise, violet, chartreuse, scarlet, even almost black! Flowers are small and hidden within the bracts. Don't feed these plants, and you can throw away insecticides; leaves are too tough for insects. For specific descriptions and culture see:

Aechmea	Guzmania
Ananas	Hohenbergia
Billbergia	Neoregelia
Bromelia	Nidularium
Catopsis	Portea
Cryptanthus	Tillandsia
Dyckia	Vriesia

BROUGHTONIA   *Orchidaceae* 55-75**F**

A charming 4- to 6-inch epiphytic orchid with colorful cerise flowers all winter. Leaves are dark green and leathery. Grow in 4-inch pots of osmunda or fir bark; provide sun and water, and the plant will otherwise take care of itself. Flowers are tiny replicas of the popular cattleya corsage orchid. Seedlings from suppliers.

B. sanguinea

BRUNFELSIA   yesterday-today-and-tomorrow

Solanaceae 60-68**F**

A fine but difficult-to-grow, winter-blooming plant to 36 inches. It bears pretty, fragrant purple flowers that turn white about a week after opening. Foliage is green and bushy. Grow in bright light and keep soil evenly moist; 50 per cent humidity. If you have trouble with this one, try a large pot, say 6- to 8-inch, and keep pinching shoots back when young; put in shady garden in summer. Propagate by stem cuttings in spring.

B. calycina floribunda

Burro's tail see SEDUM

Button fern see PELLAEA and FERNS

Butterfly orchid see ONCIDIUM and ORCHIDS

CACTUS

The cactus family is extensive. Although all cacti are succulents, not all succulents are cacti. Cacti offer the indoor gardener an array of unusual forms and brilliant blossoms. There are small types that stay small for years, perfect for windows, large kinds if you have space for them.

Most cacti have spines or scales that reduce evaporation of stored moisture during the long dry spells of their native lands. Many are from the desert; they rest in winter, grow in summer. This type needs porous soil and well-drained containers just big enough to hold them. Don't overpot, and repot only every second or third year in fresh soil but usually in the same container, since plants grow very slowly. In summer and spring, keep soil evenly moist; in fall and winter, allow it to become somewhat dry, but never bone-dry.

The orchid cactus (*Epiphyllum*), mistletoe cactus (*Rhipsalis*), Thanksgiving or crab cactus (*Zygocactus truncatus*), Easter cactus (*Epiphylopsis* or *Rhipsalidopsis gaertneri*), and the Christmas cactus (*Schlumbergera bridgesii*) are not from the desert. They are jungle plants, mostly epiphytic; they need a mixture of leaf-mold, sand, and shredded osmunda. Be sure containers have good drainage, and pot plants tightly. Keep evenly moist in spring and summer, but let dry out between waterings in fall and winter. Give full sun then, bright light the rest of the year. Cool nights (50 to 55F) are necessary to encourage bud formation in fall; and for many of them, about a month of 12-hour uninterrupted darkness is also essential. Even light from a street lamp 20 feet away will disturb the budding cycle.

Insects rarely attack cacti; leaves are just too tough. See:

Ariocarpus	Hylocereus
Astrophytum	Mammillaria
Cephalocereus	Notocactus
Echinocactus	Opuntia
Echinocereus	Pereskia
Echinopsis	Rebutia
Epiphyllum	Rhipsalis
Epiphylopsis	Schlumbergera
(Rhipsalidopsis)	Selenicereus
Gymnocalycium	Zygocactus

CALADIUM

Araceae 60-70F

A large tribe of 20- to 30-inch plants with stunning foliage. The paper-thin, heart-shaped leaves are white, or pink, red or olive-green, and many shades between. Provide shade and warmth; water well in growth; they like to be really wet; 60 per cent or higher humidity. The growing season is generally from April until October. In fall, when leaves die down, gradually reduce amount of water. When growth has completely stopped, remove tubers from pots, dry them out, and store in heavy paper bags at 60F for 2 to 3 months. Then repot, one tuber to a 5-inch container. Although you can buy mature plants at nurseries, it is easy and fun to start your own. Grand summer decoration for shaded windows or terrace borders. Here are some I have grown:

C. 'Ace of Hearts'—crimson-and-moss-green leaves.
C. 'Ace of Spades'—red veins, red-and-white marbling, green edges.
C. 'Ann Greer'—large red-bronze leaves with emerald-green tracing.
C. 'Edith Mead'—dark-green-and-white leaves, red veins.
C. 'Gray Ghost'—creamy-white-and-green.
C. 'Pinkie'—delicate pink leaves with red veins.
C. 'Red Chief'—scarlet foliage.
C. 'Stacy'—large white-and-pink leaves.

CALATHEA

Marantaceae 60-80F

Fine foliage plants from Brazil, these are prized for their decorative green leaves, marked or striped with other colors. They need good light and plenty of water. Give them heat and high, to 80 per cent, humidity. These are not easy but they have such beautiful foliage, they are worth extra care. Many kinds are available and new ones are introduced frequently. Propagate by division at repotting time.

C. bachemiana—to 16 inches, gray-green leaves marked dark green.
C. concinna—to 20 inches, outstanding leaf contrast—dark green feather design running into deeper green, purple underneath.
C. leopardina—to 12 inches, waxy green foliage with contrasting darker green.

39 Left to right: *Calathea, Podocarpus macrophylla,* and *Aglao-nema commutatum.* U.S.D.A. photo

C. lietzei—to 24 inches, light green leaves, purple beneath.

C. makoyana—to 48 inches, a fine foliage plant; olive-green-and-pink leaves veined silver.

C. roseo-picta—to 12 inches, dark-green-and-red leaves.

C. vandenheckei—to 30 inches, white-and-dark-green foliage.

C. veitchiana—to 48 inches, leaves with a peacock-feather design—brown, chartreuse, green, and red.

C. zebrina—to 36 inches, dark velvety leaves with chartreuse background.

CALCEOLARIA pocketbook-plant
Scrophulariaceae 50-60F

These funny little plants with dark green leaves and puffy pouch flowers are colorful annuals. When flowering is over, you have to discard them, but even so they are desirable. Usually a gift plant, if kept cool and shaded with even moisture at the roots, it will stay fresh for 2 to 3 weeks. Sow seeds in April or August for new plants; seedlings need cool growing.

C. herbeohybrida—to 24 inches, bushy compact ball of color, usually yellow or red with spots.

C. multiflora—to 16 inches, yellow flowers in terminal clusters.

* *nana*—to 10 inches; popular dwarf sold as gift plant.

Calico-flower see ARISTOLOCHIA

Calla-lily see ZANTEDESCHIA

CAMELLIA

Theaceae 45-60F

Don't believe these cannot be grown indoors. If you have a fully light or sunny place (three to four hours), where night temperatures are between 45 and 55F and days rarely above 60F, you will be amazed at the flowers you can have, in winter on some varieties, in spring on others. For potting, use 2 parts garden loam, 1 part acid peatmoss, and 1 part sand. Acidity is essential, pH 5 to 5.5. Give plenty of water, soil should never dry out, and mist foliage every day in summer, about every other day the rest of the year. Apply an acid fertilizer during active growth in spring and keep humidity about 60 per cent then. Repot only when absolutely necessary. Indoors, watch for occasional attacks of scale or mealy bugs, but if plants are grown cool with good air circulation, there is little danger of pests. To assure bloom, put plants outdoors in summer. Bud-drop or buds failing to open are complaints of some hobbyists; too much water in cool weather hinders bud opening, and too little water will cause bud dropping. Most camellias are tall, to about 48 inches, ideal as floor plants in front of cool windows or for sun porches or plant rooms. New plants by seed, cutting, or layering. Most nurseries carry *C. japonica* and *C. sasanqua* varieties.

C. japonica—This group produces large flowers in a wide range of whites, pinks, and reds. A long season of bloom—five to seven months—also makes them desirable.

'Colonel Fiery'—double crimson flowers from January on.

'Debutante'—crested pink single flowers, October to January.

'Elegans'—peony form, red-and-white flowers in January.

'Pink Perfection'—flat pink double blooms, November to April.

'Purity'—pure white double blooms, November to April.

C. sasanqua—These offer a profusion of small flowers in the period from October to April. There are single fragrant whites, also pink and cherry-red varieties.

'William S. Hastie'—a good single crimson, February to April.

CAMPANULA star-of-Bethlehem

Campanulaceae 50-60F

For basket or bracket, these rewarding plants with trailing stems to 20 inches, are covered with white or blue flowers from August until December; a healthy specimen has hundreds of blooms. Campanulas need fresh air and good light; shade them only in summer. Fertilize when plants are in active growth, and let soil dry out between waterings. In winter, when growth slows, depending upon species, cut back to about 5 inches, continue on the dry side and keep cool (55F). Come spring, repot in fresh soil and increase moisture. Pick off flowers as they fade; seed formation reduces bloom. Take cuttings for new plants.

C. elatines alba plena—double white, "star-of-Bethlehem."

florepleno—double blue.

C. fragilis—single pale blue blooms.

C. isophylla alba—most popular, single snow-white "star-of-Bethlehem."

mayii—single larger intense blue flowers.

Candelabra aloe see ALOE

Cape-jasmine see GARDENIA

Cape-primrose see STREPTOCARPUS and GESNERIADS

CAPSICUM red-pepper-plant

Solanceae 55-60F

Delightful Christmas gift plant with spring flowers followed by autumn fruits—some shaped like miniature peppers that hold through Christmas. Give full sun and an evenly moist soil and do grow cool; fruit drops in a hot room. Although this annual lasts only a season, the colorful plants are still worth while, especially for the holidays. Propagate by seeds in spring.

C. frutescens

'Christmas Candle'—to 24 inches, broad spreading plant, slender conical yellow-to-red fruit up to 3 inches long.

'Piccolo'—to 26 inches, variegated foliage with some leaves almost white; starry lavender blooms and black-purple berries.

'Robert Craig'—to 30 inches, green foliage, white flowers and conical red fruit.

'Weatherillii'—to 30 inches, shiny green leaves, white flowers, large conical yellow-to-red fruit that hold a long time.

CARISSA   Natal-plum
Apocynaceae 55-65F

A spiny, but not thorny, vining shrub to about 2 feet indoors, with small glossy green leaves and scented white flowers followed by red berries, most decorative in all seasons for a bracket. Plants need full sun, evenly moist soil, and frequent misting of foliage to help maintain 50 per cent humidity and assure flower buds. Water sparingly when plants rest in winter. Propagate by cuttings.

C. grandiflora nana compacta

Carnival orchid see ASCOCENTRUM and ORCHIDS

Carolina-jessamine see GELSEMIUM

Carrion-flower see STAPELIA

CARYOTA   fishtail palm
Palmaceae 55-75F

Thirty-six-inch palms from tropical Asia and Australia with graceful, glossy green, scalloped foliage on tall stems. Although the zigzag leaf edges turn brown with age, the plant is most decorative, a fine palm for the house, grows slowly, and is worth while. Give bright light and keep soil evenly moist. New plants from offsets or division.

C. mitis—clusters of green fan-shaped leaves.
C. plumosa—bright green leathery fronds on a dominant trunk.

CASSIA   senna or shower-tree
Leguminosae 55-75F

Upright 36- to 50-inch plants indoors with yellow cascades of flowers in spring and summer. Great as a specimen for a patio or floor plant in front of a sunny window. In growth, give plenty of water. In winter, store like an oleander in a frostfree place with less light. New plants from cuttings.

C. corymbosa—pairs of leathery leaflets with open clusters of flowers.
C. splendida—oval leaflets, large golden flowers in racemes.

Cashmere bouquet see CLERODENDRUM

Cast-iron-plant see ASPIDISTRA

CATOPSIS
Bromeliaceae 55-75F

Easy-to-grow terrestrials with bottle form and spikes of white or yellow flowers. Pot in equal parts of osmunda and soil and place at your sunniest window. In summer, flood with water; the rest of the year grow somewhat dry; 50 to 60 per cent humidity. New plants from offsets.

C. berteroniana—to 20 inches, vase-shaped, apple-green leaves and yellow flowers.
C. floribunda—to 14 inches, dark green leaves, white-and-yellow blooms.

Centipede plant see MUEHLENBECKIA

Century-plant see AGAVE

CEPHALOCEREUS   old-man cactus
Cactaceae 55-75F

Long white hairs and a barrel shape characterize these familiar 12- to 30-inch desert plants. Since they seem to thrive almost untended, you may want one for your indoor garden. They need a sandy soil kept barely moist, tight potting, and sun. Slow-growing and impervious to time. Propagate by seeds.

C. chrysacanthus—blue-ribbed stems with yellow spines, rosy-red flowers.
C. palmeri—white hairy plant, purplish flowers.

40 *Ceropegia woodii.* Merry Gardens photo

C. senilis—long gray hairs, a curiosity, rosy bloom.

CEROPEGIA   rosary-vine
Asclepiadaceae   55-60F

Fascinating vines, sometimes to 6 feet, with heart-shaped leaves and insignificant flowers; they grow best in an airy place. More bizarre than beautiful, with tiny tubular flowers, they are novelties. Give full sun and let soil dry out between waterings. New plants from cuttings.

C. barklyi—to 18 inches, fleshy dark green leaves, purple-brown flowers.
C. caffrorum—to 20 inches, wiry vine with green-and-purple blooms.
C. sandersonii—to 20 inches, small green leaves, twining succulent growth, green flowers.
C. stapeliaeformis—to 26 inches, dark green foliage, strong succulent stems, white flowers marked with purple.

C. woodii—to 20 inches, "string-of-hearts," with heart-shaped leaves on trailing threadlike stems, pink or purple blooms with small tubers at the ends of the stems.

CESTRUM   jessamine   *Solanaceae*   55-75F

These shrubs are for scent with red or white flowers borne on and off throughout the year. Foliage is bright green. Grow in a sunny window and keep soil evenly moist; 50 per cent humidity. Plants grow large; some become specimens to 6 feet. Prune drastically to keep in bounds; even small ones bloom. Propagate by cuttings in spring.

C. nocturnum—to 6 feet, the "night-jessamine," glossy green leaves, fragrant star-shaped white blooms open in the evening.
C. parqui—to 3 feet, the "willow-leaved jessamine" with greenish white flowers, best one for indoors.

90

Chain cactus see RHIPSALIS and CACTUS

Chain fern see WOODWARDIA and FERNS

Chain-plant see TRADESCANTIA

CHAMAEDOREA (COLLINIA)   palm
Palmaceae   55-75F

Rather showy, shade-loving palms from Central America and northern South America with single or multiple trunks. Graceful for porch, patio, or pedestal stand. Give plants bright light and keep soil evenly moist. Provide 50 per cent humidity. New plants from seed.

C. cataractarum—30-inch rosette, compact with dark green fronds.
C. elegans—2 to 6 feet, the "parlor palm"; fast grower with dark green fronds.
C. erumpens—20- to 30-inch rosette, the "bamboo palm."
C. graminifolia—to 5 feet, light green slender leaflets, horizontal type.

Chenille-plant see ACALYPHA

Chilean-jasmine see DIPLADENIA

Chin cactus see GYMNOCALYCIUM and CACTUS

Chincherinchee see ORNITHOGALUM

Chinese banyan see FICUS

Chinese-evergreen see AGLAONEMA

Chinese-fan palm see LIVISTONA and PALMS

Chinese primrose see PRIMULA

CHLOROPHYTUM   spider-plant
Liliaceae   50-75F

Fine 36-inch plants that can be neglected and still survive. With grassy green leaves, some on pendent stems, these are excellent for baskets. Large pots are best as roots quickly fill containers. Mature specimens bear tiny white flowers on tall stiff stems in winter. Don't cut these off as leaf clusters form after the flowers. Give light and let soil dry out between waterings. Strong ropelike roots store water, a safety measure if you forget the plants. Propagate by removing stem runners or by division. Or cut plants apart with a sharp knife.

C. bichetii—green-and-white striped leaves.
C. comosum picturatum—yellow-and-green.
  variegatum—green leaves with white margins.
C. elatum—most popular, with glossy green foliage.

Christmas cactus see SCHLUMBERGERA and CACTUS

Christmas fern see POLYSTICHUM and FERNS

CHRYSANTHEMUM
Compositae   55-65F

With yellow, white, bronze, or red flowers, these are popular year-round gift plants to about 20 inches. To make them last for weeks, put in a cool place with morning or afternoon sun. Keep soil evenly moist. After flowers fade, cut back stems to 2 inches and set plants in a frostfree garage or coldframe with soil kept barely moist until spring. Then set out permanently in the garden.

C. frutescens

Cineraria see SENECIO

CISSUS (VITIS)
Vitaceae   50-75F

These pretty ambitious trailers or climbers to 5 feet or more—unless pruned—are among the easiest vines for an indoor planter, basket, or bracket, thriving even in an apartment. Grow in sun or shade, and allow soil to dry out between waterings. Repot every year or two; they thrive in fresh soil. Propagate by cuttings or division.

C. antarctica—"kangaroo-vine," fresh shining green leaves with brown veins.
C. discolor—velvety green leaves with red veins and tintings of white and pink, toothed edges.
C. quadrangularis—four-winged fleshy rich green stems, needs winter rest.

91

C. rhombifolia—most familiar, "grape-ivy," metallic green brown-veined foliage.
* *C. striata*—miniature type with bronze-green leaves.

CITRUS   lemon, lime, and orange trees
Rutaceae 55-60F

Fine ornamental trees to 6 feet; excellent for tub growing. Foliage is dark green and shiny, the branching habit attractive. Grow in a cold sunny enclosed porch or plant room. Water heavily when plants are in flower or fruit; at other times keep them rather dry. Fragrant blossoms open sporadically throughout the year. To get fruit, pollinate the blooms with a small paintbrush. Check for spider mites; mist foliage to prevent attacks. Acid soil necessary so use a vinegar solution or an acid fertilizer. Propagate by cuttings in spring.

C. aurantifolia—handsome spiny lime tree; you can prune for a lovely bonsai form.
C. Limonia Meyeri—"Meyer lemon," semi-dwarf and spreading, suitable for pots.
ponderosa—popular lemon tree with dark green oval leaves, best in a tub.
C. taitensis—dwarf orange, the "Otaheite," good pot plant.

CLERODENDRUM   glory-bower
Verbenaceae 50-65F

Free-flowering, these have been overlooked by indoor gardeners, yet they offer a wealth of color for little effort. The vining growth, 4 to 6 feet long, is attractive; the foliage lush green; the spring, summer, sometimes fall flowers, just grand. Give full sun and keep soil evenly moist except in winter when plants naturally lose some leaves and need little water. Don't try to force them into growth then. Decorative as pot plants or in baskets. Cuttings root easily and bloom the first year or grow from seeds.

C. bungei—"Mexican hydrangea" opens in September, rose-red marvelously fragrant flowers.
C. fragrans pleniflorum—"Cashmere bouquet," scented double pale-pink-and-purple blooms in early fall.
C. speciosum—rose-pink flowers in summer.

C. thomsoniae—white-and-deep-crimson flowers in spring.
C. ugandense—bright blue flowers from winter to spring.

Cliff-brake fern see PELLAEA and FERNS

Climbing-fern see LYGODIUM

CLIVIA   Kafir-lily
Amaryllidaceae 55-70F

Growing to 30 inches, these aristocrats among pot plants make a striking picture in bloom in April and May. Leaves are ornamental, the vivid tubular flowers exciting. Plants bloom best when pot-bound so supply 5-, 6- or 7-inch containers. Although they tolerate sun, they bloom better in light shade. Water heavily during growth, not so much the rest of the year. New plants by division of clumps.

C. Belgian Hybrids—excellent with broad leaves and very large orange-red flowers.
C. miniata—most popular, with dark green strap leaves to 18 inches, orange-colored blooms.
C. nobilis—strap leaves, pendulous red-and-yellow green-tipped flowers.
C. Zimmerman Hybrids—salmon, orange, or red blooms.

Clock-vine see THUNBERGIA

Club-moss see SELAGINELLA

Cobweb houseleek see SEMPERVIVUM

CODIAEUM   croton
Euphorbiaceae 60-80F

Striking multicolored foliage makes these splendid accent plants that grow to 3 feet or more. Foliage form varies, and colors run from pale yellow to pink, orange, red, and brown, with many shades of green. To grow these well, give them attention. Set them where there is good air circulation and 2 to 3 hours of sun. Keep soil evenly moist, except in December and January; then decrease watering somewhat. Maintain high humidity, to 70 per cent; watch out for red-spider mites. Propagate from cuttings. There are countless cultivars.

C. 'America'—maroon, oak-leaf type.
C. 'Cameo'—delicate pink.
C. 'Gloriosa'—large, broad red-purple-maroon leaves.
C. 'Harvest Moon'—broad yellow-and-green foliage.
C. 'Monarch'—brilliant red.
C. 'Spotlight'—narrow green-yellow-and-red leaves.
C. 'Sunday'—orange-yellow-red foliage.

COELOGYNE

Orchidaceae 50-60F

These cool-growing epiphytic orchids with pendent scapes of white, beige, or green flowers perform even better at home than in the greenhouse. Some of them grow all year, others need a month of rest with only occasional watering before, and then again, after blooming. Grow plants in fir bark kept evenly moist except as noted; give bright light but no sun and provide 40 to 60 per cent humidity. Specimen plants sometimes bloom twice a year. These are impressive flowers, sure to please. New plants from specialists.

C. *cristata*—to 20 inches, 3-inch crystal-white flowers in January and February; needs rest period.
C. *flaccida*—to 16 inches, 1-inch beige flowers in winter or early spring; needs rest period.
C. *massangeana*—to 36 inches, dozens of 1-inch beige flowers in spring, sometimes again in fall; no rest needed.
* C. *ocellata*—to 10 inches, a charmer with pretty 1-inch white-and-orange blooms; needs rest period.
C. *speciosa*—to 14 inches, 3-inch beige flowers usually in winter; no rest needed.

COFFEA Arabian coffeeplant

Rubiaceae 50-70F

An evergreen shrub that grows to 15 feet in its native land. Indoors, this makes a superior pot plant to about 3 feet with glossy green leaves and red berries in summer. Give bright light and keep soil almost wet; 30 to 50 per cent humidity. Propagate by cuttings.

C. *arabica*

COLEUS painted-leaf-plant

Labiatae 55-65F

Old-fashioned favorites, these easy-to-grow plants to 16 inches are valued for their colorful foliage—plum, red or pink, green or yellow. Grow in a bright place, water every second or third day and they will grow luxuriantly. If you put them outside in summer, you will be rewarded with blue flowers. Watch out for mealy bugs. New plants from seed. Cultivars appear frequently. These are good varieties of C. *blumei*:

C. 'Brilliancy'—red-and-gold foliage.
C. 'Candidum'—large broad wavy leaves, yellow-green and white.
C. 'Christmas Cheer'—wine-red leaves edged yellow-green.
C. 'Firebird'—orange-red edged green.
C. 'Forest Park'—red-and-light-green leaves.
C. 'Pink Rainbow' — red-and-moss-green with red veins.
C. 'Sunset'—salmon-rose with moss-green areas.
C. 'The Chief'—ruffled bright red, outstanding.

COLOCASIA elephant-ears or taro

Araceae 60-80F

These have always been among my favorite house plants. The large green velvety leaves on tall stems are so elegant. Keep plants in a bright place, water heavily in growth. In winter when plants are dormant, carry them almost dry in pots at 60F. New plants from tubers.

C. *antiquorum illustris*—to 48 inches, green foliage with purple spots.
C. *esculenta*—to 40 inches, quilted satiny green leaves.

COLUMNEA

Gesneriaceae 55-70F

Columneas are beautiful trailers, climbers, or upright plants to 36 inches. Foliage varies in size, color, and form but it is always decorative. Some have tiny button leaves, others elliptical 1- to 6-inch foliage. The tubular 1- to 3-inch flowers are borne in leaf axils and may be yellow, red, orange, or pink. Since plants are epiphytic, growing on trees in their native land, use an orchid mix—1 part fir bark or osmunda

to 1 part soil. Columneas need about the same amount of light as African-violets, a rather sunny window in winter and a shaded place in summer. Keep soil evenly moist and fertilize (10-10-5) every other week during active growth. Keep humidity high, about 70 per cent. Propagate by tip cuttings.

C. arguta—trailer, dainty pointed leaves, large salmon-red flowers.

C. microphylla—trailer, tiny leaves, red-and-yellow blooms.

C. tulae flava—climber or trailer, soft green leaves, bright yellow flowers.

Some good new varieties:

C. 'Anna C'—dark red flowers, a basket plant.

C. 'Butterball'—yellow flowers on an upright grower.

C. 'Eagles'—orange blooms, semierect plant.

C. 'Early Bird'—orange-red flowers, a trailer.

C. 'Yellow Dragon'—yellow flowers, a trailer.

C. 'Yellow Gold' — darker yellow blooms, a trailer.

Comet orchid see ANGRAECUM and
ORCHIDS

Common fig see FICUS

CONVALLARIA   lily-of-the-valley
Liliaceae   50-65F

Familiar garden plants grown for their sweet
fragrance. For indoors, in fall, buy "forcing
pips," and plant in pots or bowls of sphagnum
moss or soil. Keep either medium evenly moist.
Grow in a dim place for about ten days gradually bringing to light and sun. Flowers open
almost exactly in 21 days; for Thanksgiving,
plant November 3; for Christmas, December 3;
for Valentine's Day, January 23. Roots lifted
from the garden in October, potted and kept
cool and fairly dry, also produce blooms indoors towards spring but these cannot be so
exactly scheduled as "forcing pips."

C. majalis

Coralberry see ARDISIA

CORDYLINE (DRACAENA)   ti-plant
Liliaceae   55-75F

Palmlike growth at the top of a trunk makes
these graceful plants most attractive. They are
easy to grow in 4- or 5-inch pots in a bright
airy spot. Keep soil moderately moist except in
winter; then grow cool (55F) and quite dry.
The miracle "Hawaiian log" that comes to life
in a dish of water is a member of this family.
Check for aphids in leaf axils. Propagate by
stem cuttings.

C. banksii—to 3 feet, dark green strap leaves
with pale yellow midrib, drooping panicles of
white flowers.
C. terminalis—to 3 feet, the popular "ti-plant"
with yellow, white, or reddish flowers; many
with brilliant leaves:
  'Bicolor'—dark metallic green leaves edged
  pink.
  'Firebrand'—compact rosette of red leaves.
  'Margaret Storey'—green-to-copper foliage
  splashed red and pink.

Cornplant see DRACAENA

COSTUS
Zingiberaceae   55-75F

From Central and South America come these
charming plants with succulent stems and spectacular, large, paper-thin, open-faced flowers,
appearing in spring or summer, even in fall.
Plants need sun, evenly moist soil, and about
50 per cent humidity. Propagate by dividing
clumps in spring.

C. igneus—to 36 inches, shiny green leaves,
3-inch orange flowers.
C. malortieanus—to 36 inches, "stepladder
plant," green banded leaves, orange-and-red
flowers.
C. speciosus—to 5 feet, the "spiral ginger,"
white flowers with yellow centers and red
bracts.

COTYLEDON
Crassulaceae   60-75F

South African succulents of sculptural form
with highly-colored leaves and vivid pendent
flowers. (Small species have been placed in the
genus *Adromischus*.) Give plants full sun, an
evenly moist soil, and good air circulation.
Don't water from overhead; moisture on foliage coupled with dark days causes leaf-rot.
New plants from leaf or stem cuttings in spring.

C. orbiculata—to 36 inches, frosty red leaves
and red blooms.
  * *ausana*—to 12 inches, silvery leaves, red
  flowers.
C. teretifolia—to 36 inches with 10-inch clusters of dark green hairy leaves, yellow blooms.
C. undulata—to 36 inches, waxy white foliage,
orange-and-red flowers.

Crab cactus see ZYGOCACTUS and
CACTUS

CRASSULA
Crassulaceae   55-75F

Crassulas are ideal house plants. Having fleshy
leaves and stems, they tolerate lack of moisture
in air and soil. Some have gray or blue foliage;
others are green. Several have branching stems,
many produce low rosettes of leaves. Bright
light or full sun suits them; let soil dry out

42 (Above left) *Crassula fulcata*; (Above right) *C. rupestris*;
(Below) *C. schmidtii*. Merry Gardens photos

between waterings. New plants from seed or stem or leaf cuttings.

C. argentea—to 5 feet, branching stems of glossy leaves.
* *C. cooperi*—to 5-inches, small pointed leaves with dark markings.
C. falcata—to 4 feet, thick gray sickle-shaped leaves.
C. rupestris—to 16 inches, triangular gray-green leaves.
* *C. schmidtii*—to 6-inches, pointed red-tinted leaves.

Creeping Charlie see PILEA

Creeping fig see FICUS

CRINUM   angel-lily
Amaryllidaceae 50-65F

Forty-inch tropical and semitropical plants with evergreen foliage and lovely fragrant flowers, these grow fast and bloom freely in summer. Plant in March with half the bulb above the soil. Water heavily *after* growth starts. Shade lightly from hot sun and mist foliage frequently. After they flower, move plants to a shaded location and water moderately. Repot only every 3 or 4 years. Propagate by offsets.

C. 'Cecil Houdyshel'—one of the best, lovely pink flowers.
C. 'Ellen Bosanquet'—striking with dark rose-colored flowers.
C. moorei—pink bell-shaped blooms.
C. powellii alba—beautiful white form.

Crocodile aloe see ALOE

Crocus see CHAPTER 5

CROSSANDRA
Acanthaceae 55-70F

This splendid indoor grower to 30 inches is becoming very popular. The shiny green-leaved plant bears orange flowers on and off throughout the year. Give sun and an uncrowded place at the window; keep well watered in spring, give less moisture the rest of the year. New plants from seed.

C. infundibuliformis

Croton see CODIAEUM

Crown cactus see REBUTIA and CACTUS

Crown-of-thorns see EUPHORBIA

CRYPTANTHUS   starplant
Bromeliaceae 55-75F

Small with striking foliage and waxy white flowers, it is the rosetted leaves that make the plant worth while. They are often prickly, always vibrantly colored in shades of copper, gold, silver, or bronze. Undemanding, plants need only bright light and 3- to 4-inch pots of osmunda kept evenly moist. Lovely decorative accents for terrariums and dish gardens; pot plants can endure drought for months. New plants from offsets.

* *C. acualis*—to 10 inches, apple-green foliage.
C. bahianus—to 10 inches, rosettes of recurved wavy-edged dark red leaves.
* *C. bivittatus*—to 8 inches, a dish-garden favorite with salmon-rose, olive-green leaves.
C. bromeloides tricolor—to 14 inches, "rainbow-plant"; smooth white, rose, and olive-green leaves.
C. fosterianus—to 14 inches, dark-brown-and-silver-banded rosette.
C. terminalis—to 12 inches, erect bronze-tinted foliage.
C. zonatus—to 12 inches, wavy brown-green leaves with silver markings.

CTENANTHE
Marantaceae 55-75F

This genus offers some fine foliage plants with stiff upright variegated leaves. Grow in bright light and keep soil evenly moist. New plants by division.

C. lubbersiana—to 24 inches, yellow-mottled green leaves.
C. oppenheimiana—to 36 inches, stiff white-and-green foliage.
     tricolor—tufted pink, white, and green leaves.

CYANOTIS
Commelinaceae 55-70F

To 10 inches, with gray-green foliage, these are hardly showy plants but desirable for their purple-and-orange blooms in spring. Give full sun and keep soil evenly moist. Propagate by cuttings at any time.

* C. kewensis—"teddy-bear plant," succulent creeper with hairy velvety brown foliage.
* C. somaliensis—"pussy-ears," triangular glossy green leaves with white hairs.

CYCAS   fern- or sago-palm
Cycadaceae 55-75F

Tough slow-growing plants, these look like a cross between palm and fern. Although cumbersome, a well-grown specimen with dark leathery green foliage is indeed handsome. Grow in bright light in sandy soil kept evenly moist except in winter when plants are not in active growth. New plants by division.

C. circinalis—the "fern-palm," to 6 feet, shiny dark green leaves.
C. revoluta—the "sago-palm," to 5 feet, leaves rolled on edges.

CYCLAMEN   shooting-star
Primulaceae 45-60F

These cool-preference plants, sometimes called the "poor man's orchid" are charming with shooting-star flowers, pure white through rose, pink, salmon, and scarlet. The pretty dark-green mottled leaves are heart-shaped, the single, double, and fringed blooms, some quite dazzling, go on opening for three to four months. Mainly gift plants, they last only if you grow them *cool* and moist and shade them from the sun. Mist tops frequently. Feed plants every other week and inspect foliage for cyclamen mite. Use a hard spray of water to eradicate any pests. When flowers fade in March or April, let the plant rest by gradually withholding water until foliage dies. Keep nearly dry, the pot on its side in a shaded place outdoors until August or early September. Then remove dead foliage and repot in fresh soil (equal parts garden loam, peatmoss, and sand). Set the top of the tuber level with the surface of the soil; otherwise water may collect in the depression and cause crown-rot. There are many handsome varieties of the species. New plants from seed.

C. persicum (giganteum)

CYPERUS
Cyperaceae 55-70F

Very satisfactory plants, the stems crowned with a fountain of leaves, they grow best in shade. Set directly in water or in soil kept quite wet. Look for little green flowers in the crowns; they appear in late summer. New plants by division.

C. altnerifolius—to 4 feet, the familiar "umbrella-plant," tall stems with green crowns.
C. elegans—to 36 inches, stiff narrow leaves.
C. papyrus—to 5 feet, the "Egyptian paper-plant" with flamboyant foliage.

Cypripedium orchid see PAPHIOPEDILUM and ORCHIDS

Daffodils see CHAPTER 5

Dancing-lady orchid see ONCIDIUM and ORCHIDS

Date palm see PHOENIX and PALMS

DATURA   angel's-trumpet
Solanaceae 55-65F

Large showy shrubs to 5 feet with attractive green leaves and 3- to 5-inch pendent pink or white trumpet flowers. Because of their size and reluctance to bloom indoors, they are rarely seen. However, if you want to try one, grow it in sun and let soil dry out somewhat between waterings; 50 per cent humidity. New plants from cuttings.

D. mollis—nodding salmon-pink flowers.
D. suaveolens—large green leaves, mammoth fragrant white blooms.

DAVALLIA   rabbit's-foot fern
Polypodiaceae 55-75F

Choice ferns with lacy fronds and brown or gray surface rhizomes; interesting and beautiful for the indoor garden. Grow in bright light and keep soil evenly moist. Mist foliage frequently. Put mature plants on pedestals so full beauty of the pendent graceful fronds can be appreciated. Propagate by division of rhizomes; cut them into sections and partially bury in sand.

D. *bullata mariesii*—10-inch fronds, creeping brown rhizomes.

D. *fejeensis plumosa*—15-inch fronds, dainty fluffy-leaved plant.

D. *griffithiana*—the same with gray-white rhizomes.

D. *solida*—24-inch stiff bright green fronds, brown rhizomes.

DENDROBIUM

Orchidaceae 45-75F

A genus of striking epiphytic orchids with 2- to 4-foot cane growth and large flowers in pink, yellow, or white. Leaves are leathery, and some of the prettiest species are deciduous. Grow at a south or west window with humidity to 50 per cent. Pot in fir bark and water heavily when plants are growing; rest plants with very little water in late October for about four to six weeks at 45 to 50F to encourage buds. After

they flower, rest plants again for about six weeks; then return to warmth (70F). Repot only if fir bark is pulverized. A wealth of color for indoors or out. New plants from specialists.

D. *dalhousieanum*—evergreen, tawny yellow flowers with crimson markings, spring or early summer.

* D. *jenkensii*—to 2 inches, golden-yellow flowers in summer and fall.

* D. *loddigesii*—to 6 inches, lavender-pink blooms.

* D. *monile*—to 8 inches, fragrant white flowers.

D. *moschatum*—deciduous, musk-scented large yellow-rose flowers from spring to August.

D. *pierardii*—deciduous, easy to grow with handsome 3-inch pink blooms in March or April.

D. *thyrsiflorum*—evergreen, magnificent 2-inch white-and-gold flowers in April or May.

DICHORISANDRA

Commelinaceae 60-75F

Good for indoor gardens with north light. From South America, these 12- to 20-inch plants bear pretty blue flowers in spring and summer. Most species need plenty of water while growing; in winter plants are usually dormant so water sparingly then. New plants from tubers.

D. reginae—small leaves with purple-and-silver markings.

D. warscewicziana—silver-streaked leaves.

DIEFFENBACHIA   dumbcane

Araceae 60-75F

Dumbcane is hardly an appropriate name for this easy group of graceful plants with large ornamental leaves marked yellow, blue, or white. Plants thrive in light shade and a mature specimen will be with you for years. Give plenty of water in summer—not so much the rest of the year. Best grown as tub plants. Propagate by stem cuttings in spring.

D. amoena—to 3 feet, heavy green-and-white foliage, robust.

D. bowmannii—to 3 feet, chartreuse mottled-green foliage.

D. picta barraquiniana—to 4 feet, bright green leaves spotted white.

D. splendens—to 3 feet, velvety green foliage with small white dots.

DIPLADENIA (MANDEVILLA)
Mexican-love-vine

Apocynaceae 60-80F

Charming climbing plants, to 7 feet or more, from the jungles of Brazil, with leathery leaves and great displays of pale pink flowers in spring and summer, sometimes into fall. Provide a sunny window, keep soil moist except immediately after flowering, then carry somewhat dry for about six weeks; 50 per cent humidity. Propagate by stem cuttings or by sowing seeds in spring.

D. amoena—dark green oblong leaves and 2-inch pink flowers.

D. suaveolens—the "Chilean-jasmine," long

44 Left to right: *Dieffenbachia picta*, **D. amoena**, and **Ficus pandurata**. U.S.D.A. photo

45   *Dracaena*. Alberts & Merkel Bros., Inc.

light green foliage and deliciously fragrant white flowers.

DIZYGOTHECA   false-aralia
Araliaceae 55-75F

Graceful treelike plants with dark green-brown palm leaves; lovely delicate accents. Plants reach to 6 feet but can be kept cut back. Grow in 5-inch pots; sometimes young plants are difficult to start, so have patience and don't overwater. Place in bright light and keep soil evenly moist. Air-layer for new plants, or to reduce height, or propagate from cuttings in spring.

D. *elegantissima*—leathery notched-ribbon metallic leaves.
D. *veitchii*—coppery-green foliage with light red veins.

Double-decker plant see RECHSTEINERIA

DRACAENA   cornplant
Liliaceae 55-75F

A genus of excellent African plants that survive untoward conditions; the dark green lance leaves are usually banded white or yellow. Most are large plants, to 5 feet; D. *marginata* and 'General Pershing' are exceedingly decorative; D. *fragrans massangeana* can be trained to grow like a small tree—most charming. Give good light but not sun and keep soil evenly moist. Don't let water accumulate on leaves; it can cause spotting. New plants from stem cuttings.

D. *fragrans*—green leaves to 36 inches with creamy yellow margins.
   massangeana—common "cornplant" with arching yellow-and-green 24-inch leaves.
D. 'General Pershing'—creamy pink, almost red, 24-inch leaves.
D. *godseffiana*—yellow-and-green 6-inch leaves.

101

D. marginata—18-inch dark green leaves, edged red.

D. sanderiana—9-inch green leaves banded white.

D. warneckii—24-inch white leaves with green center stripe.

DROSANTHEMUM

Aizoaceae 50-70F

Small orange-colored spring flowers make this succulent an attractive window plant. Grow it in sun and let soil dry out between waterings. Propagate by cuttings.

* *D. floribundum*—to 12 inches, thin drooping branches of pale green cylindrical leaves.

D. speciosum—to 24 inches, erect bright green foliage.

Dumbcane see DIEFFENBACHIA

DYCKIA earth-star

Bromeliaceae 55-75F

Carefree bromeliads with 12- to 16-inch rosettes of thick, often spiny, multicolored leaves. In good light, mature plants produce erect spikes of orange flowers. Excellent terrarium plants. Pot in osmunda, kept barely moist, and grow in bright light. New plants from offshoots in spring.

D. brevifolia—dark glossy green rosette, grows for years with little attention.

D. fosteriana—narrow arching silver leaves, brilliant accent plant.

D. frigida—large frosted green leaves, handsome.

Eagle claws cactus see ECHINOCACTUS and CACTUS

Earth-star see DYCKIA and BROMELIADS

Easter cactus see EPIPHYLOPSIS and CACTUS

ECHEVERIA

Crassulaceae 55-75F

Beautiful leaf rosettes put these plants from Mexico, central and northern South America

high on the list of desirables. Bright and cheery orange or red tubular flowers appear in spring and summer. Grow these 24- to 30-inch plants in the cactus-succulent mix (Chapter 2); give sun and keep soil somewhat dry. If you have any difficulties, try watering from the bottom. Easily propagated by seeds or offsets.

E. affinis—dark greenish black foliage, red flowers.

E. amoena—small rosette, pink flowers.

E. derenbergii—pale green foliage, orange blooms.

E. elegans—pale blue-white leaves, coral-pink blooms.

E. glauca pumila—bluish-gray rosettes.

E. multicaulis—coppery rosettes, orange blooms.

E. pilosa—hairy red-tipped rosette, orange flowers.

ECHINOCACTUS

Cactaceae 55-75F

Spiny attractive plants of cylindrical shape, these grow easily at windows. Put them in bright light and let soil dry out between waterings. Plants need fresh air and coolness in winter when they rest. New ones from offsets or cuttings rooted in damp sand. Young plants to 16 inches are best; mature specimens require too much space.

E. grusonii—to 48 inches, "golden barrel cactus," yellow blooms.

* *E. horizonthalonius*—to 10 inches, "eagle claws" silver-gray-and-pink leaves with red spines.

E. ingens—to 60 inches, barrel type, brownish-blue foliage with yellow flowers.

ECHINOCEREUS
hedgehog or rainbow cactus

Cactaceae 55-75F

Occasionally bearing bright-colored flowers at the window, these small desert cacti rarely grow more than 12 inches high and need little attention. Give them sun and keep the sandy soil somewhat dry. Propagate by offsets.

* *E. baileyi*—4-inch cylinder, lovely pink flowers.

* *E. dasyacanthus*—4 to 12 inches, small dense

spines, the "rainbow cactus," yellow blooms.
* *E. delaetii*—8 inches, long white spines, known as "lesser-old-man cactus," pink flowers.
* *E. pentalopus*—cylindrical 5-inch plant, fingerlike stems, violet-red flowers.
* *E. reichenbachii*—close-ribbed globe to 8 inches, white-to-red-brown flowers.
* *E. rigidissimus*—4 to 8 inches, also called the "rainbow cactus," multicolored spines of pink, white, red, and brown.

ECHINOPSIS   sea-urchin cactus
Cactaceae   55-75F

Globular desert plants from 4 to 16 inches high that bear trumpet-shaped spring flowers. Little care is required to coax them into bloom.

Place at a sunny window and keep soil moderately moist except in winter; then grow somewhat dry. Flowers open in the evening and last through the next day. Propagate by offsets.

E. calochlora—yellow-and-brown cactus with white blooms.
E. campylacantha—globular plant, dark grayish green with stiff spines, purple-white flowers.
E. eyriesii—brown spines and beautiful pure white lilylike blooms.
E. multiplex—barrel-shaped, dark green with brown spines, rose-colored flowers.

Egyptian paper-plant see CYPERUS

Egyptian star-flower see PENTAS

Elephant-ears see COLOCASIA

Emerald feather see ASPARAGUS

English ivy see HEDERA

EPIDENDRUM

Orchidaceae 60-80F

Free-flowering mostly epiphytic plants with two types of growth: cane-stemmed or with pseudobulbs. They bear handsome flowers in shades of pink, red, yellow, or white that last for six weeks. Grow plants in fir bark; give full sun. Keep cane-stemmed ones moist all year; rest the others for one month before and after flowering; 50 per cent humidity. Young plants from suppliers.

E. *atropurpureum*—to 30 inches, egg-shaped pseudobulbs, dozens of 1-inch brown-and-purple blooms in early spring.
E. *cochleatum*—to 30 inches, pseudobulbs 2 to 5 inches, dark-maroon-and-chartreuse seashell flowers, on and off throughout the year; rest in November.
E. *fragrans*—to 24 inches, compressed pseudobulbs, fragrant white-and-red flowers in late summer; rest somewhat in fall.
E. *lindleyanum*—to 29 inches, cane growth, rose-purple blooms with white lips, in fall.
E. *nemorale*—to 24 inches, globose pseudobulbs; 3-inch rose-mauve flowers in summer; rest somewhat in fall.
E. *o'brienianum*—to 84 inches, cane-stemmed; tiny typical orchid flowers in various shades.
E. *pentotis*—to 20 inches, with pseudobulbs; fragrant white blooms striped with purple in summer, rest somewhat in fall.
* E. *polybulbon*—to 4 inches, tiny yellow-and-brown flowers in summer.
* E. *porpax*—to 2 inches, reddish brown half-inch flowers in fall.

EPIPHYLLUM orchid cactus

Cactaceae 55-75F

Large hanging plants, mostly epiphytic, to 4 feet or upright growers (if staked) to 20 inches, famous for evening blooms, red or pink, purple or white, with peak in May and June. Hybrids have also been developed for day bloom. Keep plants potbound and in a bright window. Water heavily in spring and summer, not so much the rest of the year but never let dry out. Plants can be staked and look fine on a window sill or growing as natural trailers in baskets. Don't miss these mammoth flowers; plants *do bloom* indoors with little care and always cause comment in my garden room. Cuttings in spring for new plants.

E. 'Conway Giant'—7-inch magnificent purplish-red day blooms.
E. 'Eden'—6-inch white-and-yellow day flowers.
E. 'Luminosa'—5-inch day blooms.
E. 'Nocturne'—6-inch purple-and-white night blooms.
E. *oxypetalum*—species with 5-inch white night-blooming flowers.
E. 'Parade'—6-inch pink day blooms.
E. 'Royal Rose'—6-inch rose-buff day flowers.

EPIPHYLOPSIS (RHIPSALIDOPSIS)
Easter cactus

Cactaceae 55-70F

Somewhat similar but technically different from *Schlumbergera* varieties are these 12- to 20-inch epiphytes that bloom when very small with bright flowers—red, pink, or orange-pink. For bloom, grow in sun in fall and winter with coolness (55F) and uninterrupted darkness of 12 hours. In spring and summer, water plants freely and regularly. Humidity: 60 per cent. Propagate by cuttings.

R. *gaertneri*—the true Easter cactus; bright red flowers. Formerly *Schlumbergera gaertneri*.
R. *rosea*—small plant, soft pink flowers in spring.
'Orange Spring Beauty'—delicate color for early spring.

EPISCIA peacock-plant

Gesneriaceae 65-80F

Colorful 14- to 20-inch South American epiphytes with exotic foliage and brilliant flowers in spring and summer. Mostly trailers, plants need bright light, copious amounts of water, and 50 per cent humidity. If conditions are good, they grow through winter without dormancy. Keep water off leaves to avoid spotting. New plants from seeds, cuttings, or offshoots.

E. 'Acajou'—bright silver foliage and red flowers.

E. 'Cameo'—glossy metallic rose-red leaves and orange-red flowers.

E. 'Chocolate Soldier'—dark-brown-and-silver-gray leaves, red flowers.

E. *cupreata*—copper foliage dusted with white hairs, scarlet flowers.

E. *dianthiflora*—green velvety leaves and tufted white flowers.

E. 'Emerald Queen'—green leaves, red flowers.

E. 'Frosty'—white leaves and red flowers.

E. *lilacina*—coppery foliage, lavender blooms.

E. *punctata*—toothed green leaves, white flowers spotted purple.

E. 'Silver Streak'—bronze-green-and-silver leaves, red flowers.

ERANTHEMUM   blue-sage
Acanthaceae   50-70F

One of the nicest true-blue winter-flowering plants for the window garden. Give full sun and keep soil evenly moist; 40 per cent humidity. Overwatering will cause leaf drop. Small plants flower as readily as large ones. Propagate by root cuttings in spring and summer.

E. *nervosum*—to 36 inches, pointed green leaves, deep blue flowers.

E. *wattii*—to 24 inches, green leaves with metallic sheen, violet-blue flowers.

EUCHARIS   Amazon-lily
Amaryllidaceae   55-75F

Most desirable, this glossy green 40-inch bulbous plant bears fragrant starry white flowers once or twice a year. Give it bright light and flood with water in summer; after it blooms, keep it rather dry for a few weeks; then start the cycle again. To produce bloom, mist foliage frequently; feed moderately. New plants by division of clumps.

E. *grandiflora*

EUCOMIS   pineapple lily
Liliaceae   50-70F

Interesting bulbous plants to 30 inches with shiny green foliage and handsome crowns of flowers in July or August. Give the growing plants bright light and keep soil moderately wet; in winter, when plants are semidormant, grow almost dry. Propagate by offsets or sow seeds in spring.

E. *comosa (punctata)*—dark green leaves and star-shaped greenish white-and-purple flowers; lovely curiosity.

E. *undulata*—bright green leaves and a dense head of bright green flowers, striking.

E. *zambexiaca*—light green foliage, airy white flowers.

EUGENIA   rose-apple or Surinam-cherry
Myrtaceae   50-65F

Lovely small trees that can be kept to 3 feet for indoors; great accent in front of floor-to-ceiling windows. The leaves are attractive, flowers pretty, and the red berries ornamental. Provide full sun and keep soil evenly moist. New plants from cuttings.

E. *jambos*—"rose-apple" tree, pointed smooth green leaves, greenish-yellow flowers.

E. *uniflora*—"Surinam cherry," glossy leaves, white flowers and red berries.

EUPHORBIA   crown-of-thorns
Euphorbiaceae   50-75F

Most of the easy-to-grow plants in this group have small leaves and develop contorted forms; the poinsettia (see the next description) has large leaves. They need full sun and quite sandy soil kept evenly moist but never soggy. Plants resent drafts. Propagate by cuttings.

E. *keysii*—to 30 inches, a hybrid with coral-pink flowers in winter and spring; succulent leaves.

E. *lactea cristata*—to 24 inches, crested cactus-like desert species with candelabra form.

E. *splendens*—to 24 inches, the familiar "crown-of-thorns," a spiny climber; tiny green leaves and red blooms.

'Bojeri'—dwarf form, paler green leaves.

EUPHORBIA PULCHERRIMA   poinsettia
Euphorbiaceae   55-65F

The "flowers" are actually the highly-colored leaves—red, pink, or white—the tiny blooms being hidden in the center of the bracts. This is usually a Christmas gift plant but there is no reason why it should not become a year-round plant for you. When you receive it, put it in a sunny but cool window (65F). Water every other day until the leaves start to fall. Then reduce moisture until the soil is almost dry and move the plant to a semishaded window at about 55F and water it about once a month. In late March or early April, cut it back to about 6 inches and repot in fresh soil. Water well and place in a sunny window until the weather is warm outdoors. Then put it in the garden in a bright location and keep the soil evenly moist. In September, bring it back into the house, give more water and sun. From late September on, this plant must have a period of uninterrupted darkness, at least 12 hours and 14 hours would be better, to initiate flower buds. Moving plants to a closet at night insures that no beam from a street light or turned-on table lamp will break up the necessarily long period of darkness.

E. *pulcherrima*—These Mikkelsen varieties hold foliage and bracts for 3 to 6 months:
'Mikkeldawn'—variegated pink and cream.
'Mikkelpink'—nice clear color.
'Mikkelwhite'—not so strong as others but very pretty.
'Paul Mikkelsen'—brilliant red.

EXACUM German-violet
Gentianaceae 50-65F

With small fragrant blue flowers and shiny green leaves, this 24-inch plant starts flowering in September and reaches its peak in January. Give full sun and keep soil evenly moist. Cut back in August to insure future bloom. Propagate by seeds.

E. *affine*

Fairy primrose see PRIMULA

False-aralia see DIZYGOTHECA

False-holly see OSMANTHUS

FATSHEDERA   *Araliaceae* 55-75F
Shrubby pot plants with green or variegated leaves on a central stem that needs the support of a stake. These hybrids, a cross between an English ivy and a fatsia, are excellent for church rooms and offices since they can survive poor light and low humidity. Foliage develops best color without sun; soak and allow to dry out before watering again. New plants from cuttings.

F. *lizei*—to 36 inches, dark lustrous green leathery leaves.
variegata—to 36 inches, fresh green leaves edged white.

FATSIA
Araliaceae 55-75F

A group of undaunted decorative plants with dark green ivy leaves on graceful stems. Plants withstand almost any conditions and survive for years. Give shade and keep soil wet but not sodden. These will grow in a shaded entry or other interior area where most plant would perish. New ones from seed.

F. *japonica*—to 5 feet, leathery dark shining green leaves.
variegata—to 5 feet, medium-green leaves edged with white.

Fern-palm see CYCAS

FERNS
Ferns were popular house plants years ago and now, once again, their natural grace and handsome fronds are recognized as superb decoration. Grow at a cool, light, rather than sunny window, although some winter sun is acceptable, and in moist humusy soil. I use one part loam to one part each of sand, peatmoss, and leafmold. Once a week shower plants in sink or tub and at least once a month give a deep soaking so all roots get moisture. Take care to avoid standing water, as in a jardiniere, for this is most harmful to roots. Summer plants outdoors; they love warm, not cold, refreshing rains. While some gardeners feed ferns, I have found mine do very well without additional food. Try not to break or brush against the delicate fronds; if bruised at tips, they turn brown. Trim away any dead leaves and train plants to emphasize their natural grace. Elevate procumbent types on inverted pots or stands, or grow them in baskets for good effect. Many

47 (Above left) *Davallia fejeensis* (rabbit's-foot fern); (Right) *Asplenium bulbiferum* (mother fern); (Below left) *Polystichum aculeatum* (hedge fern) (Right) *Polypodium aureum glaucum* (hare's-foot fern). Merry Gardens photos

ferns can be propagated from the seeds or spores as they are properly called. These appear, usually in a pattern, on the underside of the fronds and are not to be confused with scale, which they resemble. Check plants regularly for scale; a strong water spray will sometimes eradicate the pests; if not, use the appropriate insecticide. See culture under these headings:

Adiantum	Phyllitis
Asplenium	Platycerium
Blechnum	Polystichum
Davallia	Pteris
Nephrolepsis	Woodwardia
Pellaea	

Fishtail palm see CARYOTA and PALMS

FICUS　　fig or rubber-plant
　　　　　　　　　Moraceae 60-75F

These are almost perfect house plants with diversified foliage and growth. Some like *F. elastica decora* are erect with broad leathery 12-inch leaves; *F. pumila* is a creeping plant with 1-inch leaves; *F. benjamina* forms a small tree with 2-inch oval leaves. Grow plants in bright light and keep soil evenly moist except in winter when they can get along with less moisture. Small pots are best even for large plants. Occasionally, wipe foliage with a damp cloth to keep it shiny but avoid clogging leaf pores with oil or special leaf-polishing preparations; plain water will do. Propagate by leaf cuttings or air layering.

F. benjamina—to 5 feet, the "weeping fig," with a dense head of gracefully drooping branches.
F. carica—to 4 feet, the common fig, with big green leaves; plant loses foliage during winter.
F. diversifolia—to 3 feet, the "mistletoe fig," bears small round yellowish fruit.
F. elastica decora—to 5 feet, the popular "rubber-plant," with thick glossy green leaves.
F. lyrata (pandurata)—to 5 feet, the "fiddle-leaf fig," with enormous leaves; avoid drafts that cause leaf drop.
F. pumila (repens)—"creeping fig," with 1-inch leaves, often used as a soil cover for big pot plants.

F. retusa—to 5 feet, the "Chinese banyan," a slow-growing tree with dark green leaves.

Fiddle-leaf fig see FICUS

Fig see FICUS

FITTONIA　　　　　*Acanthaceae* 60-75F

Low dense creepers from the forests of Peru with soft bright green, 4-inch leaves veined red or white. Plants need shade; keep out of drafts and let soil dry out between waterings; 50 per cent humidity. Grow several kinds in one container for a colorful display. Good for dish gardens and planters. Stem cuttings root easily.

F. verschaffeltii—leaves with red veins.
　　argyroneura—leaves with white veins.

Flame-of-the-woods see IXORA

Flamingo-flower see ANTHURIUM

Flaming-sword-plant see VRIESIA and BROMELIADS

Flowering maple see ABUTILON

Flowering onion see ALLIUM

Fox-tail orchid see RHYNCHOSTYLIS and ORCHIDS

FREESIA
　　　　　　　　　Iridaceae 50-60F

Tender bulbous plants with delightfully fragrant flowers, difficult to grow indoors but not impossible. Put six corms, 1 inch deep and 2 inches apart in a 5- or 6-inch pot of two parts sandy loam, one part leafmold, and one part old manure or compost. Plant from August to November for January to April bloom. Keep them cool and moist, and give full light. Flowers appear in 10 to 12 weeks. After plants bloom, gradually dry out the soil and then shake out the corms and keep dry for repotting next year. Propagate by offsets.

F. 'Blue Banner'—sky blue with white throat.
F. 'Gold Coast'—orange-colored flowers.
F. 'Stockholm'—carmine.

FUCHSIA   lady's-eardrops
Onagraceae 50-65F

Handsome plants, some trailing, others upright to 3 feet, with small dark green leaves and dangling red, white, pink or purple flowers. Their beauty depends on considerable care. Grow in rich soil out of sun but in bright light and below 65F. Then they will set flower buds in spring and summer; feed biweekly. Flood while they are growing; pinch at early stages to encourage branching. Mist foliage frequently and provide a buoyant atmosphere. While they are dormant in winter, carry almost dry in a cold dim place. Watch out for white fly. Take cuttings in January or February.

F. 'Brigadoon'—trailer, double purple-and-pink flowers.

F. 'Carmel Blue'—trailer, single blue blooms with white sepals.

F. 'Cascade' trailer, single rose-red with white sepals.

F. 'Dark Eyes'—trailer, double violet-blue blooms.

F. 'Marenga'—trailer, variegated foliage, double red flowers.

F. 'Mrs. Marshall'—upright, single soft pink flowers with white sepals.

F. 'Sleigh Bells'—upright, large single pure white blooms.

F. 'Swingtime'—trailer, fine double white flowers with red sepals.

F. 'Tiffany'—trailer, double white.

GARDENIA   Cape-jasmine
Rubiaceae 60-70F

Evergreen shrubs with scented waxen white flowers and shiny dark green leaves. They are difficult to bloom at home, but adjusting slowly to new conditions, they are not impossible. Grow in equal parts loam, sand, and acid peatmoss. Keep soil evenly moist. Give bright light in summer, sun in winter, and 50 per cent humidity at least. From spring to fall, feed once a month with an acid fertilizer or a solution of 1-ounce ammonium sulphate to 2 gallons of water. (Applying the vinegar-and-water solution, ½ teaspoon to 1 quart of water, will acidify soil but not feed the plant.) Mist foliage daily to discourage red spider. Give a deep

soaking in the sink or in a pail of water once a week and a refreshing shower at the same time. Buds may drop or fail to open if night temperature is above 70 or below 60; if temperatures fluctuate very much; if there are drafts; if humidity is below 50 per cent. If your plant does not grow or is ailing, try the plastic-bag method for a few weeks. Cover the plant with plastic held above the foliage by stakes and tied at the base. Propagate by cuttings in spring.

G. jasminoides—to 4 feet, double white blooms.
   'Veitchii'—to 4 feet, smaller flowers but easier to grow.
   stricta nana—to 30 inches, free flowering, best for the home.

Garland-flower see HEDYCHIUM

GASTERIA   ox-tongue plant
Lilaceae 55-75F

Interesting South American succulents for window sills or almost any exposure. The long flat leaves are usually smooth, but sometimes "warted"; long sprays of scarlet bloom appear in spring and summer. Grow in sun and water lightly. Propagate by offsets.

G. carinata—5- to 6-inch triangular fleshy leaves, flower spike to 36 inches.

G. lingua—10-inch dark green leaves with white spots, inflorescence to 36 inches.

G. maculata—8-inch glossy green leaves, inflorescence to 48 inches.

G. verrucosa—6- to 9-inch pink-and-purple leaves with 24-inch flower spikes.

GAZANIA
Compositae 50-70F

Colorful plants to 30 inches with large black-eyed yellow-to-orange daisy blooms and long, narrow, woolly gray-green foliage. Flowers open in sunlight and close at night. Excellent for a cool sun porch where plants will bloom on and off through spring and summer. They need lots of water but do not require high humidity. Propagate from seeds or cuttings.

G. rigens—typical species with golden-yellow flowers, brown-black center.

G. splendens—orange flowers.

109

GELSEMIUM   Carolina-jessamine
Loganiaceae 55-75F

A choice twining shrub to 40 inches with tiny fragrant funnel-shaped yellow flowers through the winter. Grow in a sunny place and keep soil evenly moist. Propagate by cuttings or seeds.

G. sempervirens

Geranium see PELARGONIUM

German-violet see EXACUM

GESNERIADS

African-violets are well-known and now other gesneriads are enjoying popularity, and rightly so for they offer brilliant color indoors. In baskets, *achimenes, aeschynanthus, columneas, episcias,* and *hypocyrtas* are veritable cascades of bloom. *Gloxinias, rechsteinerias, sinningias, smithianthas,* and *streptocarpus* are best grown as pot plants. The main requirement for all of them is high humidity, at least to 70 per cent. While some thrive at 70F, others require it cool (58F). Most gesneriads do not need much sun, but rather a place with bright light and good air movement. Plants do well in a loose soil mixture that holds moisture yet drains readily. In general, plants are healthy and not prone to disease. See culture under each heading:

Achimenes	Rechsteineria
Aeschynanthus	Saintpaulia
Columnea	Sinningia
Episcia	Smithiantha
Hypocyrta	Streptocarpus
Kohleria	

Ginger see ALPINIA, ZINGIBER

Ginger-lily see HEDYCHIUM

GLORIOSA   glory lily
Liliaceae 55-75F

Splendid climbing plants with narrow green leaves and exquisite orange-and-yellow lilies in spring and summer. Sure to bloom, they require little attention. Plant one tuber to a 5-inch pot; growth will appear in two weeks. Provide a bamboo stake for plant to climb on. Give sun, plenty of water, and 50 per cent humidity. Propagate by seeds or tuber division in spring.

G. rothschildiana—to 6 feet, large to 3-inch orange-and-yellow flowers edged with crimson. *G. simplex (virescens)*—to 4 feet, broader petals, 2-inch orange-and-yellow blooms.

Glory-bower see CLERODENDRUM

Glory-lily see GLORIOSA

Gloxinia see SINNINGIA and GESNERIADS

Gold-dust-tree see AUCUBA

Golden bamboo see BAMBUSA

Golden barrel cactus see ECHINOCACTUS and CACTUS

Golden calla see ZANTEDESCHIA

Gold-spined aloe see ALOE

GONGORA   Punch-and-Judy orchids
Orchidaceae 60-80F

Large curious epiphytes with pairs of 20-inch green leaves and pendent scapes of tawny yellow flowers; these grow better at a window than in a greenhouse. Give diffused sun. Pot in fir bark and keep moist except in winter when plants can be grown almost dry; 50 per cent humidity. Propagate by division.

G. bufonia—broad pale green leaves, dozens of 1-inch flowers in summer.
G. galeata—1-inch blooms from June to September.

Grape-hyacinths see CHAPTER 5

Grape-ivy see CISSUS

Grecian-urn-plant see ACANTHUS

GREVILLEA   silk-oak
Proteaceae 55-75F

Fast-growing, with delicate foliage, these make good large floor plants and they almost take care of themselves. Merely place in sun and give plenty of water. Propagate from seeds.

G. *bipinnatifida*—to 4 feet, with loose racemes of red blooms.
G. *wilsonii*—to 5 feet, needle leaves, curious red-and-yellow flowers.

Ground-ivy see NEPETA

GUZMANIA
Bromeliaceae 55-75F

Striking plants with rosettes of leaves and small flowers hidden in vivid bracts that stay colorful for 4 months. Give bright light; pot in osmunda and keep wet but never soggy; 50 per cent humidity. Fine table decoration. New plants from specialists.

G. *berteroniana*—20-inch rosette of wine-red leaves, yellow flowers in spring.
G. *lingulata*—26-inch rosette of apple-green leaves; star-shaped orange inflorescence all summer.
G. *monostachia*—26-inch rosette with red, black, and white flower-head in fall.
G. *musaica*—20-inch rosette of dark-green-and-red-brown leaves, white flowers in fall.
G. *zahnii*—20-inch rosette of green leaves, red-and-white flowers in summer.

GYMNOCALYCIUM   chin cactus
Cactaceae 55-75F

Interesting desert cacti to 12 inches, with white or yellow or chartreuse flowers that usually open in spring and summer. Grow in sun in sandy moist soil. Propagate by offsets.

* G. *mihanovichii*—depressed 2-inch gray-green globe with yellowish white flowers.
* G. *quehlianum*—6-inch globe, white-and-red flowers.
* G. *schickendantzii*—4-inch globe, white or pinkish flowers.

GYNURA   velvet-plant
Compositae 65-75F

A popular ornamental with large purple leaves. Grows rapidly to 30 inches. Give sun and frequent watering; humidity 40 to 60 per cent. This is an unusual plant; the foliage almost glows with color. Desirable for planter boxes or where special accent is needed. Propagate by cuttings.

G. *aurantiaca*

HAEMANTHUS   blood-lily
Amaryllidaceae 55-70F

Ornamental bulbous plants with luxuriant fleshy leaves and hundreds of tiny flowers in a sphere. Pot one bulb with tip protruding in a 5- or 7-inch container. Top-dress with fresh soil at start of each growing season. Repot only once in 3 or 4 years. Plants need sun and plenty of water in summer. In winter, keep soil nearly dry. Propagate by offsets when bulbs are repotted in fall or spring.

H. *coccineus*—to 10 inches, spectacular red flowers in fall; plants dormant in summer.
H. *katherinae*—to 12 inches, evergreen with salmon-red blooms in spring after foliage develops.
H. *multiflorus*—to 18 inches, red flowers in spring before foliage develops.

Hardy amaryllis see LYCORIS

Hare's-foot fern see POLYPODIUM

Hartford-fern see LYGODIUM

Hart's-tongue fern see PHYLLITIS and FERNS

HAWORTHIA
Liliaceae 55-75F

Small foliage plants from South Africa (they resemble aloes) with rosettes of stiff leaves, brown or green or purple-brown. Some are erect, others are low growers. Carefree plants, they thrive in shade. Give plenty of water in summer; less moisture the rest of the year.

111

Good for dish gardens. Propagate by seed.

* *H. fasciata*—small erect rosette, with 1½-inch dark green incurved leaves banded with white.
* *H. margaritifera*—low-growing rosettes 6 inches across with 3-inch sharply pointed leaves with white granules; dense sprays of flowers to 2 feet.
* *H. retusa*—stemless clustered rosette with 1½-inch pale green flat leaves.
* *H. viscosa*—erect rosette to 8 inches with 3-inch dull green rough leaves.

HEDERA   ivy
Araliaceae 50-60F

Trailing or climbing plants with many leaf forms—all attractive. Bright decoration for brick walls in a plant room or in baskets or trained in topiary forms. Equally good for a pot trellis. But don't try to grow ivy in a warm room; coolness and humidity are keys to success. Give plants bright light rather than sun. Soak soil, then let dry, then soak again. Give overhead spraying in the sink at least once a week, and an occasional soapy wash is necessary to keep plants free of aphids and spider mites. Provide 30 to 50 per cent humidity. Propagate by cuttings any time.

H. canariensis—"Algerian ivy," large fresh green leathery leaves, slightly recurved.
H. helix—"English ivy"
　'Goldheart'—gold center, green edges.
　'Green Ripples'—pleated leaves.
　'Itsy Bitsy'—tiny pointed leaves.
　'Jubilee'—green and white.
　'Manda's Crested'—wavy five-point leaves.
　'Shamrock'—compact small leaves.

Hedge fern see POLYSTICHUM

Hedgehog or rainbow cactus see
ECHINOCEREUS and CACTUS

HEDYCHIUM   ginger-lily
Zingiberaceae 55-75F

Large plants to 6 feet with canes of pale or glossy green leaves and fragrant white or yel-low flowers in summer. Excellent for tubs in a sunny corner or outdoors on a terrace. Give plenty of water and up to 50 per cent humidity. Reduce moisture after blooming is over. Propagate by dividing tubers in spring.

H. coronarium—"garland-flower," sweetly-scented pure white flowers.
H. flavum—"yellow ginger," luxuriant pointed green leaves, yellow flowers.
H. gardnerianum—"Kahili ginger," 18-inch leaves with red-and-yellow flamboyant blooms.

HELICONIA
Musaceae 55-75F

The banana family offers some large plants with showy tropical flowers and leathery leaves. Give sun, rich soil kept evenly moist, and 50 per cent humidity. Difficult to make bloom, still worth the space required because if flowers do come, they are superb. Less water in winter, a time of natural rest. Good patio decoration or for a plant room. Propagate by dividing rootstock when growth starts in spring.

H. angustifolia—to 36 inches, 2-foot leathery leaves, orange-red bracts.
H. aurantiaca—to 30 inches, smooth foliage topped with orange-and-green bracts.
H. psittacorum—"parrot-flower," to 24 inches, rich green leaves, orange bracts, greenish yellow flowers, best one for window growing.

Heliotrope see HELIOTROPIUM

HELIOTROPIUM   heliotrope
Boraginaceae 55-75F

An old-fashioned favorite with white, lavender, or dark purple flowers—often deliciously fragrant—from January until summer. To 40 inches, this makes a good standard. Plants need sun, a rich soil, and even moisture. Watch out for white fly. Propagate by cuttings or seed.

H. arborescens—vanilla-scented violet flowers.
　'Marine'—semidwarf to 20 inches with purple flowers.
　'First Snow'—pure white.

Hen-and-chickens see SEMPERVIVUM

HIBISCUS   rose-of-China

Malvaceae   55-75F

Large free-flowering plants to 4 feet for sun porch or plant room with single or double blooms in red, yellow, pink, or white, opening on and off throughout the year. Grow in 10- to 12-inch pots in full sun with plenty of water; these are thirsty plants; 30 to 50 per cent humidity. Feed moderately. Prune back hard in early spring; plants grow quickly. Watch out for red-spider attack. Stand pot in pail of water once a month for a good soaking. Propagate by cuttings.

H. rosa-sinensis
   'Agnes Goult'—large single rose blooms.
   'California Gold'—large single ochre-yellow flowers.
   cooperi—variegated foliage, small red blooms.
   'Scarlet'—green leaves, intensely red flowers.
   'Snow Queen'—variegated foliage, small pink flowers.
   'White Wings'—white blooms, stained red.

HIPPEASTRUM   amaryllis

Amaryllidaceae   55-65F

Striking bulbous plants with strap foliage and mammoth flowers in white, pink, red, rose, or violet, the throats lighter or darker, petals sometimes banded, striped, or bordered in a contrasting color, the stalks up to 26 inches. Buy quality bulbs in late fall. Plant and start into growth from January to March. Allow one bulb to a 6- or 7-inch pot, always with 1-inch space between the walls and the bulb. Don't bury the bulb; let the upper third reach above the soil line. Moisten soil, set pot in a cool dark place, and grow almost dry until the flower bud is up 6 inches or more. Then move into sun and water heavily. From planting to blooming is generally three weeks or more. After a plant blooms, keep it growing so leaves can manufacture food for next year's flowers. When foliage turns brown, let soil go almost dry for about 3 months, or until you see a new flower bud emerging; then replant in fresh soil but, if possible, in the same container. If you have a garden, set plant out when danger of frost is past, plunging it into the soil.

As weather turns cool in fall, bring indoors to about a 55F place. Water lightly, only enough to keep leaves from wilting, until you start plants into a new cycle of growth. Propagate by seeds or offsets.

H. 'Claret'—8-inch flowers, crimson on wine color with red-black lines.
H. 'Giant White'—7-inch glistening flowers.
H. 'Pink Perfection'—7-inch rose flowers, lighter petal tips, the throat dark carmine.
H. 'Peppermint'—8-inch white-and-red striped blooms.
H. 'Scarlet Admiral'—7-inch glossy red blooms.
H. 'Winter Joy'—5-inch red flowers with darker throat and orange-red petal tips.

HOFFMANNIA

Rubiaceae   50-75F

Splendid foliage plants from Mexico with velvety leaves in glowing green and dark red. They grow well at a north window; keep soil evenly moist. Good for planters or wherever a bright accent is needed. Propagate by cuttings.

H. *ghiesbreghtii*—to 4 feet, brown-green foliage.
H. *refulgens*—to 15 inches, almost iridescent crinkled leaves, edged magenta and rose.
H. *roezlii*—to 30 inches, copper-brown-and-bronze foliage.

HOHENBERGIA

Bromeliaceae   55-75F

Striking plants that need space. Broad golden-green leaves in rosettes to 48 inches across and erect spikes of vivid lavender-blue flowers to 40 inches. Pot in osmunda. Grow in full sun and keep the vase of the plant filled with water; 30 to 50 per cent humidity. Attractive for a terrace. Plants are spiny; wear gloves when handling them. New ones from specialists.

H. *ridleyii*—golden-yellow rosette, lavender flower crown.
H. *stellata*—golden-green leaves, violet-flower-head.

Holly fern see POLYSTICHUM and FERNS

Honeybells see MAHERNIA

113

HOWEA (KENTIA)   Kentia palm
Palmaceae   55-75F

Indestructible foliage plants to 5 feet, decorative, with graceful fronds. Grow in semishade and keep soil evenly moist. Plants do best when potbound so provide only 6- or 8-inch containers even for mature specimens. Soak plant in a pail of water once a month to keep in good health. Propagate by offsets.

H. belmoreana—"sentry palm," strongly arching very sharply-pointed fronds.
H. fosteriana—"paradise palm," broader hanging waxy dark green fronds.

HOYA   waxplant
Asclepiadacea   55-75F

Attractive vines to 4 feet or more with leathery, glossy leaves and charming clusters of very fragrant flowers. Only mature plants 4- to 5-years-old are likely to bloom, young ones rarely. Plants need full sun and will not bud at all in shade. Grow potbound and give plenty of water in spring, summer, and fall; in winter let soil go almost dry. Don't remove stem or spur on which flowers have been produced; this is also source of next season's bloom. Mist foliage frequently and check for mealy bugs. Best grown on a trellis or support but can also be handsome hanging from a basket. Propagate by cuttings in spring.

H. bella—to 20 inches, "miniature waxplant," tiny leaves, umbels of purple-centered white blooms.
H. carnosa—to 4 feet, familiar "waxplant," white flowers with pink centers.
H. 'Compacta'—to 12 inches, with white flowers.
H. keysii—to 30 inches, gray-green leaves, white flowers.
H. motoskei—to 4 feet, oval leaves with silver spots, pink blooms.

Hyacinths, Dutch and French-Roman see CHAPTER 5

HYDRANGEA
Saxifragaceae   55-70F

Familiar Easter pot plants, these large-leaved shrubs have showy clusters of white, blue, or pink flowers. Keep soil almost wet, sometimes watering more than once a day. Grow cool, not over 70F in sun with plenty of fresh air; humidity 30 to 50 per cent. After plants bloom, cut back shoots to two joints; repot in slightly acid soil and set outdoors; feed biweekly and keep well watered. After the first frost, store indoors where it is cool, about 45F, and dim. Keep soil barely moist; water about once a month. In January, increase warmth, light, and water. When plant is actively growing, move to a 60 to 65F window. The degree of soil acidity determines the coloring of the pink and the blue varieties. A pink plant can be made blue by changing the soil to an acid 5.0 to 5.5 pH.

H. macrophylla
'Merveille'—carmine-rose.
'Soeur Therese'—pure white.
'Strafford'—rosy red.

HYLOCEREUS   night-blooming cactus
Cactaceae   55-75F

Huge vining jungle plants to 7 feet, usually epiphytic, produce slow-opening, mammoth white flowers on summer nights, an occasion for a party because blooms last only 12 to 24 hours. To some, hardly worth the trouble of the other 364 days but to me the annual spectacle makes care worth while. (Smaller plants with smaller flowers are found among *Epiphyllum* hybrids.) *Hylocereus* plants need sun in summer and lots of water, bright light in winter with less moisture and a cooler place, about 50F. Established plants are really no trouble if you have space for them and the yearly blossoming *is* exciting. New plants from cuttings in spring.

H. undatus

HYPOCYRTA
Gesneriaceae   60-80F

Trailing epiphytes to 24 inches from Central America with tiny leaves and pouch flowers.

114

IX VARIETY IN BEGONIAS. (Upper left) 'Otto Alfred', one of the fine rhizomatous types. (Upper right) 'Fred D. Scripps', a tall branching plant for accent. Both from the author's collection. *Joyce Wilson photos.* (Lower left) An unfailing angel-wing begonia. (Lower right) The floriferous 'Christmas Candle'. *Park Seed Co. photos*

X Upper left: 'Better Times', an attractive large-flowering zonal. Upper right: The fancy-leaved 'Mme Langguth' is always appealing. *Wilson Bros. photos.* Lower left: 'Lady Pink', a lovely shade. Lower right: Carefree geraniums in many shades are easy to grow from seed. *Park Seed Co. photos*

XI LONG-BLOOMING GESNERIADS. (Above) Episcias, colorful in flower and leaf. *Park Seed Co. photo* (Below) African-violets, 'Briar' Rose' and the lavender 'Shooting Star'. *Fischer Greenhouses photo*

XII GRACEFUL PENDENT PLANTS. Above: The ivy-leaved geranium in a hanging basket. *Wilson Bros. photo* Below left: The decorative fast-growing *Asparagus sprengeri* for a tub on a stand. *Park Seed Co. photo* Below right: An indoor fern, *Pteris tremula,* often planted in with gift poinsettias. *Walter J. Haring photo*

48 *Hypocyrta strigillosa.* Merry Gardens photo

Plants need winter sun and summer shade; 60 per cent humidity. Set on brackets or grow in hanging baskets in equal parts of shredded osmunda and soil. After they bloom, some kinds rest for a few months; grow them almost dry then. Flowers come in brilliant shades of orange and red. After they fade, prune plants back to encourage branching; new blooms appear on new growth the following fall and winter. Propagate from tip cuttings of new growth.

H. nummularia—a creeper with vermilion-yellow-violet flowers. May go dormant in summer but leafs out again in fall.
H. strigillosa—spreading semierect habit with reddish-orange flowers.
H. wettsteinii—pendent grower with orange-yellow flowers on and off throughout the year.

IMPATIENS   patience-plant
                 Balsaminaceae 50-65F

Excellent window plants that offer color almost all year with pretty pink, white, orange, or red blooms. Plants need a bright place and evenly moist soil in summer; keep barely moist in winter and grow in a cool place (65F). Propagate by cuttings or seeds.

I. holstii—to 24 inches, reddish leaves and red flowers.
  * 'Orange Baby'—to 8 inches; deep orange flowers.
I. platypetala aurantiaca—to 26 inches, green foliage and salmon-orange flowers.
I. repens—to 20 inches, delightful trailer with red branches and golden yellow hooded flowers with brown stripes.

115

I. sultanii—to 20 inches, "patient Lucy," green leaves, continuous bloom, red or pink.

Inchplant see TRADESCANTIA

Indoor linden see SPARMANNIA

Ivy see HEDERA

Ivy-arum see SCINDAPSUS

IXORA   flame-of-the-woods
Rubiaceae   50-70F

Robust house plants to 36 inches with ornamental foliage and clusters of bright flowers; some plants bloom twice through early spring and summer. They need sun, a moist soil except in winter; then carry somewhat dry. Even young plants bloom; a worth-while group. Propagate by cuttings.

I. chinensis—4-inch leaves, red-to-white-blooms.
I. 'Gillette's Yellow'—floriferous, with sunny flowers.
I. javanica—7-inch leaves, willowy branches, orange-red flowers.
I. 'Super King'—compact and free flowering, 6-inch ball-shaped flower clusters, blooms twice.

JACARANDA
Bignoniaceae   50-75F

A fine small tree to 36 inches with ferny growth rather like that of mimosa; ideal for sun nook or pedestal table; plant grows rapidly with little care. Give a bright location and keep soil evenly moist. Blue-violet panicles may appear in spring or summer, but rarely flowers indoors. Easily grown from seeds.

J. acutifolia

Jacobean-lily see SPREKELIA

JACOBINIA   king's-crown
Acanthaceae   50-75F

From Brazil, to 30 inches, these plants have downy green leaves and plumes of pink or orange flowers; charming for summer color. Grow at a sunny window with good air circulation and keep soil wet; insufficient moisture causes leaf drop. Take tip cuttings in spring for new plants, discard old ones.

J. carnea—upright with dark green leaves, pink flowers.
J. ghiesbreghtiana—light green leaves, orange blooms.
J. suberecta—spreading growth, hairy foliage, orange flowers.

Jasmine see JASMINUM

JASMINUM   jasmine
Oleaceae   55-65F

Every indoor garden becomes fragrant with jasmine. One large vining plant perfumes a whole room from March (sometimes earlier) to November. Some kinds get large, others reach only to 12 inches. With dark green leaves and yellow or white flowers in clusters at the branch tips or in leaf axils, these slow-growing plants are worth their space in gold. Grow in sun with evenly moist soil, 50 per cent humidity. Use acid fertilizer. Mist foliage occasionally and give pots a deep soaking in the sink once a month. Propagate by cuttings.

J. humile—to 6 feet, bushy with yellow flowers.
J. officinale grandiflorum—to 6 feet, "poet's jasmine," shrubby ferny vine with large white flowers.
J. parkeri—to 12 inches, with tiny yellow blooms.
J. sambac
   'Maid of Orleans'—to 3 feet, shrubby, "Arabian jasmine," with single white flowers; very fine.
   'Grand Duke'—double white flowers, less dependable but beautiful.

JATROPHA
Euphorbiaceae   50-75F

Lovely tropical evergreen shrubs to 4 feet in constant bloom in my plant room with clusters of brilliant red flowers and broad green leaves. Place in sun and keep soil evenly moist. Propagate by seeds.

J. pandurifolia
   'Dwarf'—small version of species to 24 inches.
   'Holly Leaf'—good scarlet.

Jerusalem-cherry see SOLANUM

Jessamine see CESTRUM

KAEMPFERIA   peacock-plant
Zingiberaceae 55-75F

An exquisite 12-inch plant with beautiful foliage and attractive flowers, this is not to be missed. It bears colorful lavender blooms, a few a day, all summer; leaves are almost iridescent. Grow in bright light and keep soil fairly moist but not soaked. Let tuber die down in winter and store cold in a paper bag. Repot in March or April in a 6-inch container.

K. roscoeana

Kafir lily see CLIVIA

Kahili ginger see HEDYCHIUM

Kangaroo-vine see CISSUS

King's-crown see JACOBINIA

Kentia-palm see HOWEA and PALMS

KALANCHOE
Crassulaceae 60-70F

These plants vary in type of growth and foliage, and they survive untoward conditions. They are short-day plants and will only bloom when day-length is less than 12 hours. If the short-day schedule is started in October, flowering will usually commence in about two months. Plants bought in bloom at Christmas will continue for a month or longer. The fleshy green leaves and clusters of small, showy red or orange blossoms are indeed welcome in winter. Give bright light and let soil dry out well between waterings. To avoid mildew, take care not to overwater nor to grow in a humid atmosphere. If leaves develop a white coating, dust lightly with Karathane. Use 3- or 4-inch pots and repot every second year. New plants from spring sowing of seed or by separate potting of naturally formed plantlets.

K. blossfeldiana—to 20 inches, sometimes blooms twice—in winter and again in spring.
   'Tom Thumb'—a dwarf hybrid seen in florists shops at Christmas.

K. tomentosa—the "panda plant," grown for foliage, to 20 inches with brown-spotted gray-green fuzzy leaves.
K. uniflora—to 14 inches, a charming prostrate species with pink-to-orange bell-flowers late in winter, sometimes into spring.

KOHLERIA
Gesneriaceae 60-80F

Fine trailers or upright growers with colorful tubular flowers and attractive foliage. Plants need bright light rather than sun. Water heavily in growth, much less the rest of the time, only about once a week, but never allow plants to become completely dry or they may die. Use room temperature water; cold water spots the soft furry foliage. Do not mist plants but give adequate humidity, say 60 per cent. Take tip cuttings for new plants or large rhizomes may be separated and single scales planted like seeds.

K. amabilis—to 16 inches, green leaves and pink blooms in spring and summer, basket plant.
K. bogotensis—to 24 inches, stake and grow upright, brilliant red-and-yellow flowers in summer.
K. eriantha—to 24 inches, erect grower with bright red flowers from summer to fall.
K. lindeniana—to 10 inches, erect with fragrant violet-and-white flowers in late fall.
K. 'Longwood'—upright with large spotted flowers.

Lace aloe see ALOE

Lady-of-the-night see BRASSAVOLA

Lady palm see RHAPIS and PALMS

Lady's-eardrops see FUCHSIA

Lady-slipper orchid see PAPHIOPEDILUM and ORCHIDS

LAELIA
Orchidaceae 50-75F

Showy epiphytes, many to 30 inches with leathery leaves and pink flowers in fall. Plant in fir

49 (Above left) *Kalanchoe unifolia;* (Below right) *K. pumila.*
Merry Gardens photos

bark, soak, then allow to dry out before watering again. Grow in sun; 50 per cent humidity. Young plants from specialists.

L. *anceps*—4-inch pink flowers, several to a cluster.
L. *gouldiana*—many rose-magenta flowers.
* L. *pumila*—dwarf to 8 inches with 4-inch pale rose flowers in summer or fall.

LANTANA
Verbenaceae 50-70F

Shrubby spreading plants to 20 inches with yellow, lavender, or orange blooms. Place in sun; in summer give plenty of water. In winter, after flowering, cut plants back and grow somewhat dry. Propagate by cuttings or seed. Watch out for white fly. Can be trained to an attractive standard.

L. *camara*—orange summer flowers.
L. *montevidensis*—good trailer with lavender flowers in fall and winter.

Leadwort see PLUMBAGO

Leather fern see POLYSTICHUM and FERNS

Lemon-tree see CITRUS

Lemon-vine see PERESKIA and CACTUS

Leopard-plant see LIGULARIA

Lesser-old-man cactus see ECHINOCEREUS and CACTUS

LICUALA palm Palmaceae 55-75F

Little known but lovely, this slow-growing palm to 6 feet with wide foliage fans is undemanding and thrives at almost any exposure; 50 per cent humidity. Water several times a week. A good tub plant. Propagate by seeds.

L. *grandis*

LIGULARIA leopard-plant
Compositae 50-70F

Foliage plants to 24 inches from Japan; they thrive in north light. With round variegated leaves on graceful stems, they are showy and colorful. Grow in shade and keep the soil quite moist. New plants by division of clumps.

L. *kaempferi argentea*—green leaves with creamy white margins.
  aureo-maculata—green leaves with golden flecks.

Lily-of-the-Nile see AGAPANTHUS

Lily-of-the-valley see CONVALLARIA

Lime-tree see CITRUS

Lipstick-vine see AESCHYNANTHUS (TRICHOSPORUM)

Living-rock cactus see ARIOCARPUS and CACTUS

Living-vase-plant see AECHMEA, BILLBERGIA, NEOREGELIA, and BROMELIADS

LIVISTONA Chinese-fan palm
Palmaceae 55-70F

A robust species with a solitary trunk and big fan-shaped leaves, excellent for large rooms. Can grow to 10 feet indoors if given the space. Needs bright light and an evenly moist soil. New plants from specialists.

L. *chinensis*

Lobster claws see VRIESIA and BROMELIADS

Love-plant see MEDINILLA

LYCASTE Orchidaceae 50-75F

Epiphytic or terrestrial orchids to about 2 feet with broad pleated green leaves and regal flowers in white, pink, or vivid yellow. Pot in fir bark and give plants sun and plenty of water when they are growing. Then to encourage budding, dry them out somewhat for about a month when leaves mature. After plants bloom, carry them *completely dry* for about 6- to 8-weeks but maintain 50 to 60 per cent humidity. New plants from specialists.

50   *Kohleria amabilis*, Merry Gardens photo

L. aromatica—3 to 10 fragrant yellow flowers in spring.

L. deppei—pale green flowers spotted red, winter.

L. skinneri—5-inch blush-white winter blooms.

LYCORIS   nerine or hardy amaryllis
Amaryllidaceae   50-65F

Deciduous bulbous plants from China and Japan, with grassy foliage and large striking flowers in fall or winter. Start bulbs, with nose just above the soil, one to a 6- or 7-inch pot in April or May. Water moderately until the end of summer; then flood plants and give sun. As leaf growth develops in late fall, flowers appear. In spring, leaves turn yellow and die off. Carry dry for a few months and then start into growth again. Do not repot. Propagate by offsets.

L. radiata—to 20 inches, the "nerine lily," with bright orange-red flowers, 4-inches across.

L. squamigera—to 24 inches, the "hardy amaryllis," with fragrant 4-inch lilac flowers.

LYGODIUM   climbing-fern
Schizaeaceae   50-70F

Vinelike plants to 40 inches with attractive light lacy blue-green fronds that survive almost any situation. Plants prefer shade, with a little sun in winter. Grow in loose moist well-drained acid soil. New plants from seeds.

L. palmatum—the "Hartford fern" with 4- to 7-lobed leaves.
L. scandens—2-inch feathery blue-green leaves.

Madagascar-jasmine see STEPHANOTIS

Maidenhair fern see ADIANTUM and FERNS

MAHERNIA   honeybells
Sterculiaceae   50-60F

Fragrant yellow flowers in winter and spring on 20-inch rangy plants; grows best on sun porch or in plant room. Soak soil and let dry before watering again. Good basket subject. While not spectacular, it has charm. Propagate by cuttings.

M. verticillata

MALPIGHIA   miniature-holly
Malpighiaceae   55-70F

A dwarf evergreen to 20 inches with small spiny leaves and pale pink flowers that pop out in spring and summer and stay bright and pretty for months. Needs sun and an evenly moist soil. New plants from spring cuttings.

M. coccigera

MAMMILLARIA   pincushion cactus
Cactaceae   55-75F

Twelve to 20-inch Mexican globe cacti with colorful white, red, black, or gray spines and crowns of tiny flowers mostly in late summer and early winter. These desert plants are easily grown at a bright window with water every other day in summer and about once a week in winter. Propagate by offsets.

M. applanata—dark green with creamy white blooms.
M. bocasana—white hairs and yellow blooms.

M. fragilis—"powder-puff cactus," covered with white spines, cream-colored flowers.
M. hahniana—curly white hairs and red flowers in winter.

MANETTIA   Mexican-firecracker
Rubiaceae   55-75F

Climbing plants to 2 feet with tubular yellow-tipped red flowers almost all year at a sunny window. Let soil dry out between waterings; 50 per cent humidity. This thrives when pot-bound and requires an airy location. New plants from cuttings.

M. inflata

MARANTA (CALATHEA)   prayer-plant
Marantaceae   60-80F

Ornamental foliage and the will to grow readily at north windows give these plants a top spot on my desirable list. Keep soil moist; 50 per cent humidity. Plants thrive in 4- or 5-inch pots and where there is a good circulation of air. When resting time comes in late fall, cut away old foliage; leave the more recent foliage; grow plants with soil barely moist. In January or February, resume watering. Propagate by division at repotting time or leaf-stalk cuttings.

M. arundinacea—to 4 feet, zigzag rows of gray-green arrow-shaped leaves.
M. bicolor—to 12 inches, oval dark gray-green foliage.
M. leuconeura kerchoveana—to 15 inches, the "prayer-plant," 6-inch oval glaucous leaves, pale grayish green with rows of brown and dark green spots; folds leaves at night to funnel dew down to the roots.
    massangeana—to 15 inches, smaller gray-green leaves with silver markings.

MASDEVALLIA   kite orchid
Orchidaceae   50-65F

Five- to 15-inch epiphytic or terrestrial orchids with curious triangular flowers, usually in winter, and leathery spatula leaves. Perfect for a cool north window or an aquarium garden. Plant in fir bark or osmunda and keep moist all year; these orchids have no pseudobulbs; humidity about 80 per cent. New plants from specialists.

121

51 *Maranta.* Merry Gardens photo

* *M. bella*—large yellow-and-red flowers.
M. coccinea—most popular, rose-pink to purple-magenta blooms.
M. ignea—large cinnabar-red flowers.
M. tovarensis—pure white blooms.

MEDINILLA love-plant
Melastomaceae 55-75F

A lush blue-green plant to 40 inches with stunning pendulous panicles of carmine flowers in pink bracts. Blossoming can occur any time of year but only on mature plants in 8- or 10-inch tubs. Grow in bright light; water moderately except in winter, then only twice a week; 70 per cent humidity. Propagate by seeds or buy young plants from a specialist.

M. magnifica

Meyer lemon see CITRUS

Mexican-firecracker see MANETTIA

Mexican-foxglove see ALLOPHYTON

Mexican hydrangea see CLERODENDRUM

Mexican-love-vine see DIPLADENIA

MILTONIA pansy orchid
Orchidaceae 50-70F

Popular 12- to 20-inch epiphytes with large open-faced flowers, usually white or red or shades of red, that stay fresh on the plant for a month. Pot in fir bark, keep moist but not wet; 80 per cent humidity. Obtain young plants from a specialist; many fine species in catalogues and new varieties introduced frequently.

M. candida—chestnut-brown, tipped yellow, fall blooming.
M. flavescens—yellow sepals and petals, yellow lip marked purple, summer.
M. roezlii—white flowers stained purple, summer.
M. vexillaria—lilac-rose with yellow lip; spring.
Hybrids, white-and-red with yellow-marked masks:
    'Alexandre Dumas'

'Aramis'
'Pam Pam'
'San Roberto'

Miniature flagplant see ACORUS

Miniature-holly see MALPIGHIA

Mistletoe cactus see RHIPSALIS and CACTUS

Mistletoe fig see FICUS

Moneywort see LYSIMACHIA, CHAPTER 4

MONSTERA   Swiss-cheese-plant
Araceae   55-75F

Climbing foliage plants to 6 feet or more with 24-inch perforated leaves; excellent for planters in public rooms. Grow in bright light and keep soil evenly moist; 50 per cent humidity. This grows in water almost better than in soil. Plants adjust to warmth or coolness but keep them out of drafts. Wash or wipe foliage about once a month; older plants bear unusual boat-shaped flowers. Aerial roots grow from stem nodes; cut these off if you wish. Propagate by cuttings.

M. acuminata—14-inch leaves.
M. deliciosa—36-inch leaves with slits.
M. schleichtleinii—20-inch filigreed leaves.

Moses-in-the-cradle see RHOEO

MUEHLENBECKIA   wireplant
Polygonaceae   55-75F

Small round-leaved vines effective for baskets. Plants grow rapidly into a tight mat of foliage about 12 inches across. They are sun-lovers and resent overwatering so keep soil barely moist. New plants from tip cuttings.

M. complexa—small round green leaves, terminal flowers.
M. platyclados—"centipede plant," with soft-jointed green stems and red blooms.

MURRAEA   orange-jessamine
Rutaceae   55-70F

Evergreen shrubs with glossy green ferny foliage and very fragrant clusters of white flowers in summer and fall followed by red berries; charming in bloom or out. Give sun in growth and plenty of water, though less in winter. Propagate by cuttings.

M. exotica—smells like orange blossoms.
M. paniculata—(perhaps a form of above), "satinwood," slow growing to 20 inches, also highly scented.

MUSA   banana
Musaceae   60-80F

A good accent plant with solitary trunk to 5 feet and shiny green spatula leaves. Fine porch or terrace decoration. Give winter sun and summer shade and evenly moist soil. Propagate by cuttings.

M. nana

Narcissus see CHAPTER 5

Natal-plum see CARISSA

NEOMARICA   walking iris, apostle-plant
Iridaceae   50-70F

Dependable, fragrant winter flowers on tall stalks, strap foliage. Pot in sandy soil in 4- or 5-inch shallow containers; give full sun and plenty of water. After they bloom, rest plants for about a month with scant watering. New plants by splitting rhizomes.

N. caerulea—to 30 inches, blue-and-white flowers, the best one.
N. gracilis—to 18 inches, similar to above but smaller.
N. northiana—to 36 inches, larger fragrant flowers, white-and-violet.

NEOREGELIA   living-vase-plant
Bromeliaceae   55-75F

These epiphytes with 30- to 40-inch leaf rosettes make planters glow with color for 3 months. The center of the plant turns brilliant red at bloom time but flowers are insignificant. Pot in osmunda; keep "vase" of plant filled with water and the compost just damp. Give good light and wipe leaves with a damp cloth about once a month. Propagate from suckers that appear after bloom.

52   *Neomarica gracilis.* Merry Gardens photo

N. carolinae—dark-green-and-copper leaves, unexcelled house plant, winter blooming.
  tricolor—striped foliage, white, pink, and green.
N. cruenta—upright smaller straw-colored rosette.
N. spectabilis—"painted-fingernail-plant"; tips of pale green leaves are brilliant red, summer flowering.

NEPETA ground-ivy *Labiatae* 50-70F

Tiny trailer with prostrate stems and small round leaves with white borders; occasionally bears minute mauve flowers in summer. Good as ground-cover for plants in big pots. Grow in semishade and keep soil evenly moist; in winter, grow cool and give less moisture. Makes a nice basket plant. New ones from cuttings.

* *N. hederacea*

NEPHROLEPIS Boston or sword fern
Polypodiaceae 60-80F

These ferns survive untoward conditions and are still beautiful. They are fast growing, native to the American tropics and subtropics. Most of them form a 30-inch rosette. Give winter sun, shade in summer. Keep soil evenly moist but avoid overwatering. In addition, water large plants by standing pot up to the rim in a sink of water for about an hour once a week. Ferns benefit from warm rains when temperatures outdoors are above 50F. Easily propagated from runners from the base of mature plants.

N. exaltata—fronds to 5 feet, often sold as Boston fern, bushy.
  'Fluffy Ruffles'—12-inch fronds, lacy.
  'Verona'—8-inch fronds, dwarf with lacy fronds.
  'Whitmannii'—18-inch fronds, robust and lovely.
    bostoniensis—36-inch fronds, the true Boston fern.

Nerine see LYCORIS

NERIUM oleander *Apocynaceae* 55-75F

These summer-flowering plants grow to 5 feet and require little care to produce an abundance of colorful flowers. Although young plants bloom, it is the 3- to 4-year-old tub specimens that put on a show with flowers in shades of pink, white, or red, single or double. Growth starts in March or April; it is best to repot then in fresh soil. Give plants full sun and plenty of water. After they bloom, decrease the amount of water. Prune in October or November and store in a light, cold but frostfree, place through winter with only monthly watering. Can be grown into a standard of exceptional beauty. Propagate from seeds or cuttings of tip growth in spring.

N. oleander—the common oleander, willowy branches and rose-red single flowers.
  'Compte Barthelemy'—double red.
  'Mrs. Roeding'—double salmon-pink.
  'Peachblossom'—double apricot.

New-Zealand-flax see PHORMIUM

NIDULARIUM *Bromeliaceae* 55-75F

Easy-to-grow plants with colorful foliage in 20- to 24-inch rosettes and tiny white or pink flowers in dense clusters. Excellent for planters or north windows. Pot in osmunda, grow in bright light, the vase kept filled with water; 50 per cent humidity. Wipe foliage with a damp cloth about once a week to bring out the full beauty of the leaves. Propagate by suckers.

N. fulgens—yellow-green foliage spotted dark green.
N. innocentii—a glowing purple rosette.

Night-blooming cactus see HYLOCEREUS and CACTUS

Night-blooming cereus see SELENICEREUS and CACTUS

Night-jessamine see CESTRUM

Norfolk-Island-pine see ARAUCARIA

NOTOCACTUS ball cactus
Cactaceae 55-65F

These South American cylindrical cacti are dependable with large showy yellow blooms in spring and summer; nice for dish gardens.

Plants are easy to grow with sun and small amounts of water all year. Propagate by offsets.

* *N. ottonis*—2-inch ribbed globe.
* *N. scopa*—8-inch globe with white hairs.
* *N. submammulosus*—3-inch shining green globe.

ODONTOGLOSSUM *Orchidaceae* 50-70F

Epiphytes from the cool regions of Colombia and Peru, these are for the unheated but not freezing sun porch or plant room. With leathery leaves and generally yellow-and-brown flowers, plants stay in bloom for over a month, sometimes for three months, one flower opening as another fades. Grow in fir bark or osmunda; give sun in winter, bright light in summer, plenty of water except for a 4-week rest before and then again after flowering. Mist foliage frequently and try to maintain 50 per cent humidity. Seedlings from specialists.

O. bictoniense—15-inch leaves, 24-inch flower spikes with twenty to thirty 2-inch yellowish green and chestnut-brown blooms in fall.
O. citrosmum—10-inch leaves, scapes 2- to 3-feet, pendent with fifteen to thirty 2-inch round fragrant pink flowers in spring or early summer.
O. grande—the "tiger orchid," 12-inch leaves, scapes 10 inches, erect with 5- to 7-inch yellow-and-brown flowers in fall.
O. krameri—to 8 inches, violet flowers.
* *O. pulchellum*—unique in the family, 10-inch plant with half-inch fragrant white flowers in spring.
* *O. rossii*—dwarf, to 8 inches, with 2- to 3-inch pink-and-dark-brown flowers with wavy rose-colored lip, in winter.
O. uro-skinneri—14-inch leaves, scapes 2- to 3-feet with ten to fifteen 1-inch greenish flowers marked brown, in early spring.

Old-man cactus see CEPHALOCEREUS and CACTUS

Oleander see NERIUM

ONCIDIUM dancing-lady orchid
Orchidaceae 55-80F
Mostly epiphytic spray-type orchids with leathery leaves and pseudobulbs or with cane-stemmed growth, producing large solitary flowers, or scapes with hundreds of small flowers. Grow in fir bark, in sun with 50 per cent humidity, and provide a good circulation of air. Species with pseudobulbs need a 4 week rest with very little water before and after flowering, others require constant moisture at the roots. Flowers last a long time cut and placed in a vase of water. New plants from specialists.

O. ampliatum—to 28 inches, leathery leaves and 1-inch brown-and-yellow flowers in early spring; requires a rest.
O. ceboletta—to 20 inches, dark green almost black leathery leaves, charming tiny vivid yellow-and-brown blooms in spring; requires a rest.
O. lanceanum—to 20 inches, spatula speckled leaves and fragrant yellow-green flowers in summer; grows all year.
O. papilio—to 18 inches, "butterfly orchid," large chestnut-brown-and-yellow blooms, sometimes in summer, other times in fall; grows all year.
O. splendidum—to 24 inches, hard leathery leaves and small yellow-and-brown flowers in winter; requires a rest.
O. triquetrum—to 15 inches, 1-inch purple-green-and-white flowers in fall; grows all year.
O. wentworthianum—to 30 inches, yellow-and-red-brown blooms in summer; requires a rest.

OPUNTIA prickly-pear
Cactaceae 55-75F

Some of these cacti are handsome and decorative; others are unsightly and to be avoided. Most have flat pads with spines; others form erect cylinders. Grow in sun, water about once a week, in winter, even less, and move plants then to a cold place (50F). Bloom rarely occurs indoors. Propagate by offsets.

O. brasiliensis—to 48 inches, spineless pad shaped like a beaver's tail, yellow flowers.
* *O. erinacea*—to 12 inches, erect cylinder with white spines, pink flowers.
O. linguiformis—to 36 inches, fleshy green cylinder, yellow blooms.
O. microdasys—to 24 inches, spineless pad with snow-white hairs, yellow flowers.

O. strobiliformis—to 15 inches, erect cylinder resembling a pine cone, yellow blooms.
O. vestita—to 20 inches, white woolly cylinder, red blooms.

Orange-jessamine see MURRAEA

Orange-tree see CITRUS

ORCHIDS

The graduation of orchids from greenhouse to home is still a pleasant surprise, and growers now agree that many orchids make splendid house plants, most of them easier than some of the familiar foliage plants. The majority of orchids have water-storage vessels (pseudobulbs) so if plants are not watered for a few days or even a few weeks, they survive. And, of course, few other plants produce such dramatic colorful flowers. Orchids are terrestrial (growing in soil) or epiphytic (growing on trees). Pot the terrestrials as you do other plants; for epiphytes, use fir bark or osmunda. Don't smother these beauties with warmth and humidity. Most of them thrive in average home temperatures of 68 to 72F with 30 to 50 per cent humidity. While some need sun to bloom, others bear handsome flowers in bright light. As a rule, orchids need a rest with the potting mixture somewhat dry for a month before and a month after blooming. Those that grow all year need constant moisture. Insects rarely attack orchids.

Acineta	*Laelia*
Aerides	*Lycaste*
Angraecum	*Masdevallia*
Ansellia	*Miltonia*
Ascocentrum	*Odontoglossum*
Bifrenaria	*Oncidium*
Brassavola	*Paphiopedilum*
Broughtonia	*Rhynchostylis*
Coelogyne	*Stanhopea*
Dendrobium	*Vanda*
Epidendrum	*Zygopetalum*
Gongora	

Orchid cactus see EPIPHYLLUM and CACTUS

ORNITHOGALUM

Liliaceae 50-70F

These small bulbous plants bear charming star-shaped white flowers on leafless stalks in winter; they are good window plants but also fine as cut flowers that last for days. Plant 6 or 7 bulbs to a 6-inch pan any time from September to December. Grow in full sun and keep soil evenly moist. After plants bloom let foliage grows until bulbs dry off naturally. Store them in their pots in a cool dim place until fall. Then repot in fresh soil. Propagate by offsets when repotting.

O. arabicum—to 24 inches, clusters of fragrant white flowers with black centers.
O. thyrsoides—to 18 inches, "chincherinchee" white or yellow flowers in dense racemes.
O. umbelattum—to 12 inches, "star-of-Bethlehem," satiny white flowers with green stripes.

OSMANTHUS (OLEA)

Oleaceae 60-70F

These are evergreen shrubs that make excellent house plants, the one highly valued for indoor fragrance. Give sun, keep soil evenly moist, and assure good circulation of air. Keep potbound to stimulate flower production. Propagate by summer cuttings.

O. fragrans—"sweet olive," to 24 inches, with plain green leaves and heavily-scented tiny white flowers on and off throughout the year.
O. ilicifolius variegatus—"false-holly," to 20 inches, with white-edged green leaves.

Otaheite see CITRUS

OXALIS   wood-sorrel

Oxalidaceae 55-75F

With dainty flowers and shamrock leaves, these 6- to 12-inch bulbous plants are ideal for baskets or pots. Some varieties are everblooming, others flower in winter, spring, or summer. The delicate blooms, like buttercups, are yellow, pink, red, violet, or white. Put 4 to 6 tubers about half-an-inch deep in a 6-inch pot of soil; keep fairly moist but don't water heavily until growth starts. Then feed biweekly with a liquid fertilizer and give full sun to produce abundant

53 (Below left) *Osmanthus fragrans*; (Above right) *O. ilicifolius variegatus*. Merry Gardens photo

bloom. Flowers close at night and on dull days. Summer- and fall-flowering types require a rest in winter; store them in their pots at 50F. New plants from division of tubers.

O. *bowieana*—rose-red flowers in summer; rest in winter.
O. *cernua*—"Bermuda buttercup"; yellow blooms in summer; rest in winter.
O. *lasiandra*—purple flowers in summer and fall.
O. *melanosticta*—yellow blooms in fall; rest in spring and summer.
O. *ortgiesii*—yellow flowers on and off throughout the year; no resting time.
O. *rosea*—pink flowers in spring; no resting time.
O. *rubra alba*—pink flowers in summer; rest in winter.

Ox-tongue-plant see GASTERIA

Painted-leaf-plant see COLEUS

Painted-fingernail-plant see NEOREGELIA and BROMELIADS

PALMS

With a central trunk and fan-shaped leaves or feathery foliage, these are long-lived plants that need little care. They thrive firmly potted in rich soil with some peatmoss and sand. My palm in a 6-inch pot grows better than two others in large containers. Peak growth is in spring and summer so water heavily then but not so much otherwise; however, never let soil get really dry. Give bright light and keep foliage clean by wiping leaves with a damp cloth once a week. Feed moderately, not more than once a month in spring and summer, not at all the rest of the year. Palms benefit from a summer outdoors where they can enjoy warm showers. Pests rarely bother plants. See:

> *Caryota*
> *Chamaedorea (Collinia)*
> *Howeia (Kentia)*
> *Licuala*
> *Livistona*
> *Phoenix*
> *Rhapis*

PANDANUS   screw-pine
Pandaraceae 60-75F

Years ago almost every barber shop in the Midwest had one of these plants in the window. With spiny lance leaves arranged in a spiral (hence the common name), some reach 4 to 5 feet indoors; others like those below rarely go beyond 40 inches. Grow in bright light in a warm place with soil somewhat dry. Plants dislike fluctuating temperatures. Propagate by offsets.

P. *baptistii*—stiff blue-green-and-yellow leaves.
P. *utilis*—long curving olive-green leaves.
P. *veitchii*—best for indoors, variegated recurved leaves.

Panda plant see KALANCHOE

Pansy orchid see MILTONIA and ORCHIDS

Paper-flower see BOUGAINVILLEA

PAPHIOPEDILUM   cypripedium or
lady-slipper orchid
Orchidaceae 55-75F

These terrestrial 10- to 16-inch orchids readily make the move from forest floor to indoor garden and produce flowers in glowing colors; some are warm-growers, some cool. All are desirable. Give them a shaded place and keep the potting mixture (equal parts soil and shredded osmunda) moist; 50 per cent humidity. New plants from suppliers. Fine as cut flowers or for corsages.

P. *callosum*—marbled foliage, 2-inch pale-green-to-rose flowers from winter to summer, cool-growing.
P. *concolor*—2-inch yellow flowers spotted red, early summer, warmth.
P. *fairieanum*—soft green leaves, 1-inch yellow-and-purple flowers in late summer and winter, cool-growing.
P. *hirsutissimum*—2- to 3-inch apple-green flowers with rose-colored spots in spring, warmth.
P. *spicerianum*—2-inch pale green leaves, purple-and-white blooms in winter, cool-growing.
P. *venustum*—mottled foliage, 2-inch purple-and-green blooms in spring, cool-growing.

Paradise palm see HOWEIA and PALMS

Parlor palm see CHAMAEDOREA and PALMS

Parrot-flower see HELICONIA

PASSIFLORA   passion-vine
Passifloraceae   55-75F

Handsome Brazilian vines to 6 feet that require space but reward you with exquisite large summer or fall flowers. These plants, preferably in 10-inch tubs, are for sun porch or plant room, too large for a window. Plants need sun, plenty of water, and fertilizer when they are actively growing. Rest them for about 3 months after they bloom and prune then. Cuttings taken in summer root readily for spring plants or sow seeds.

P. alata—lobed leaves, blue-and-white flowers.
P. caerulea—dark blue-and-pink flowers.
P. racemosa—breathtaking red blooms.
P. trifasciata—glowing purple-and-green foliage, blue flowers.

Passion-vine see PASSIFLORA

Patience-plant see IMPATIENS

Patient Lucy see IMPATIENS

Partridge-breast aloe see ALOE

Peacock-plant see EPISCIA, GESNERIADS, and KAEMPFERIA

PELARGONIUM   geranium
Geraniaceae   50-70F

Geraniums offer almost constant color if given full sun and grown rather cool with frequent airing and no crowding at the window. Plant in a rather firm soil mixture of three parts loam to one part sand plus a little peatmoss, slightly on the acid side, say pH 6.0 to 6.5, with some leeway in either direction acceptable. Water freely, then let dry out a little before watering again. Geraniums bloom best when potbound so grow in as small pots as possible. Martha Washington's and the ivy-leaveds rest

somewhat in winter; water them moderately then and do not feed. Feed the others every other week when they are in active growth, which is most of the time in sunny weather. Geraniums are sometimes troubled by edema; water-soaked spots appear on the leaves and cells burst when moisture collects in the plants faster than it is transpired from the leaves. *Avoid overwatering* and high humidity; don't mist the foliage. Do investigate the new Carefree geraniums that come true to type and color from seed. Vining geraniums in mixed colors can also be grown from seed. Propagate most other geraniums from cuttings taken in spring for winter bloom, August or early September for spring and summer flowering. Geraniums are usually classified in this way:

ZONALS—these are the familiar old-fashioned type with scalloped leaves and brilliant single and double flowers. Most varieties grow to about 30 inches. Some are smaller, some dwarf to about 12 inches; some miniatures to about 4 inches.

STANDARD TYPES
P. 'Apple Blossome Rosebud'—rose-edged white, fine for winter flowers
P. 'Better Times'—red flowers
P. 'Dreams'—double salmon-pink
P. 'Flare'—single salmon-pink
P. 'Harvest Moon'—single orange
P. 'Holiday'—single red with white center
P. 'Patricia Andrea'—brilliant rose color
P. 'Princess Fiat'—double, shrimp pink
P. 'Salmon Irene'—double, one of the five Irenes
P. 'Snowball'—double white
P. 'Starlight'—single white
P. 'Summer Cloud'—double white

CAREFREE GERANIUMS—a new true-to-type-and-color from seed. Do not pinch back to make bushy; plants grow thick on their own. Seeds sown in mid-February will produce blooming plants in early July in the Midwest. Colors include: three pink, five light and dark salmon, four white-edged rose-pink, two red, and one white.

FANCY-LEAVED TYPES
P. 'Crystal Palace Gem'—yellow-and-bright-green

* *P.* 'Filigree'—silver tricolor, single dark salmon-pink blooms
P. 'Jubilee'—yellow-green and red-brown
P. 'Skies of Italy'—golden tricolor

FREE-BLOOMING LARGE DWARFS—particularly good window plants for 4-inch pots because of their restricted growth habit, to about 10 inches, and their almost constant bloom.

P. 'Brooks Barnes'—single pink with dark-zoned leaves
P. 'Dancer'—single salmon, one of the largest "dwarfs"
P. 'Emma Hossler'—double, white-centered rose-pink
P. 'Mr. Evaarts'—large fast-growing double pink
P. 'Prince Valiant'—single crimson
P. 'Red Riding Hood'—double red on a bushy plant

P. 'Tu-Tone'—double shaded pink from light to dark

DWARF TYPES
* *P.* 'Capella'—forest-green foliage, double salmon-pink flowers
P. 'Epsilon'—soft pink
P. 'Goblin'—large double scarlet flowers
P. 'Lyric'—double orchid-pink flowers with white clusters
P. 'Minx'—double crimson-purple flowers
P. 'Perky'—single white-centered bright-red flowers
P. 'Pigmy'—scalloped leaves, semidouble bright red blooms.

MINIATURES
* *P.* 'Black Vesuvius'—single orange-scarlet with dark foliage.

54 *Pelargonium 'Lyric'.* **Merry Gardens photo**

131

* *P.* 'Fairy Tale'—white blooms; lavender centers
* *P.* 'Imp'—dark foliage, single pink flowers
* *P.* 'Saturn'—red flowers, dark foliage
* *P.* 'Venus'—double light pink flowers, strongly zoned foliage.

SCENTED-LEAVED—charming with delightful scent and varied foliage. Some leaves resemble maple, others look like gooseberry or even ferns.

P. crispum—lemon
P. graveolens—rose
P. odoratissimum—apple
P. tomentosum—peppermint.

IVY-LEAVED—trailing stems and glossy ivy-like foliage; colorful sight in summer with cascades of flowers. Pinch plants in late winter or early spring to encourage many shoots to grow. Good for hanging baskets.

P. 'Charles Turner'—fine double pink
P. 'Comtesse de Grey'—single light pink
P. 'New Dawn'—double rose-cerise
P. 'Santa Paula'—double lavender purple
P. 'Victorville'—double dark red

MARTHA WASHINGTON or LADY WASHINGTON—for a colorful spring display. Flowers are two- or three-color blends, whites tinged with lavender or pink, vibrant reds and deep purples. There are also some small free-blooming pansy types. Cut back plants after flowering and always grow cool (45 to 55F).

P. 'Dubonnet'—ruffled wine-red
P. 'Easter Greetings'—cerise flowers
P. 'Gardener's Joy'—blush-white with rose markings and stripes
P. 'Holiday'—ruffled white with crimson markings
P. 'Lavender Grand Slam'—deep tone and compact grower
P. 'Madame Layal'—purple and white pansy type
P. 'Springtime'—ruffled white with rose-colored throat

PELLAEA   cliff-brake or button fern
Polypodiaceae 50-65F

New Zealand and West Indian ferns with fronds of heart-shaped segments, these bear little resemblance to most other ferns. Fronds are erect or low and spreading, and plants grow to 30 inches. They make satisfactory house plants that need little care. Pot in soil with good drainage in 5- or 6-inch containers that will accommodate the fast-growing rhizomes. In nature, they prefer limestone rock but I have not found it necessary to add lime to the potting soil. Keep soil moist but avoid overwatering. Watch out for scale on both sides of the foliage. Propagate by spores.

P. rotundifolia—low and spreading with small round dark leaves, nice for baskets.
P. viridis—larger green leaflets; will climb if supported.

PENTAS   Egyptian star-flower
Rubiaceae 55-75F

With showy umbels of pink or white or rose flowers almost continuously and attractive pointed leaves, these are fine house plants if humidity can be kept to 50 per cent or more. Grow in sun with plenty of water when they are in active growth. Old plants get leggy so every year start new ones which will produce a medley of color, or take cuttings. Flowers last a long time in a vase of water.

P. lanceolata—to 30 inches with small rose flowers.
   'Orchid Star'—a hybrid with large lavender flowers.

PEPEROMIA
Piperaceae 55-75F

Outstanding foliage plants for window, table, planter, or terrarium with smooth-edged leaves and insignificant flowers. Many have vining growth, others make upright bushes. Place in bright light and water sparingly. Propagate by stem cuttings.

* *P. cubensis*—to 12 inches, waxy fresh green leaves; upright.
* *P. glabella variegata*—to 12 inches, yellow-and-pale green leaves; vining.
P. hederafolia—to 14 inches, bright silvery foliage with purple hues; vining.
* *P. maculosa*—to 12 inches, narrow gray-green leaves; upright.
* *P. metallica*—to 12 inches, small waxy brown leaves with pale green stripes; upright.

P. *obtusifolia*—to 16 inches, fleshy large oval leaves; vining.

* P. *ornata*—to 12 inches, dark green foliage with maroon lines; upright.

PERESKIA   lemon-vine
Cactaceae   55-75F

Unusual desert cacti that hardly appear as such. These have long narrow leaves, spiny stems, and mine occasionally bear greenish white or pink flowers in late summer. Plants need full sun and an airy place; water moderately all year. Propagate by offsets or cuttings.

P. *aculeata*—to 8 feet, thick oval leaves, white, yellow, or pink flowers.

P. *godseffiana*—somewhat smaller green leaves marked crimson and yellow.

PETREA   queen's-wreath
Verbenaceae   55-70F

True-blue flowers open in spring and summer on a twining 6- to 8-foot vine with brittle dark green leaves. This is a big plant that grows rapidly and makes a fine accent for a garden room. Give full sun and let soil dry out between waterings. Plants must be three or four years old before they will reward you with a real harvest of flowers, so have patience. Propagate by cuttings.

P. *volubilis*

56 (Above) *Philodendron cannifolium;* (Below) **P.** *andreanum.*
Merry Gardens photo

PHILODENDRON
Araceae 55-75F

A popular house plant for many years and still favored for shaded locations with little light, especially in apartments. Some species have medium-sized leaves, others large; many are vining plants and several have rosette growth ("self-heading"). The majority thrive with soil kept evenly moist and an occasional misting of leaves. Favorite planter subjects for public places. Propagate by cuttings.

P. andreanum—to 36 inches with 10-inch dark green leaves; vine.
P. bipinnatifidum—to 30 inches with 8-inch dark green scalloped leaves; vine.
P. cannifolium—20-inch rosette; lance-shaped leaves on short stems.
P. cruentum—to 20 inches, 8-inch leaves; vine.
P. erubescens—to 24 inches, 10-inch dark green leaves; vine.
P. hastatum—to 36 inches, 10-inch arrow leaves; vine.
P. imbe—to 24 inches, 10-inch leathery maroon leaves; vine.
P. oxycardium—to 36 inches, 10-inch leaves; vine.
P. selloum—to 30 inches, 15-inch notched leaves; rosette.
P. verrucosum—to 24 inches, 8-inch multicolored heart-shaped leaves; vine.
P. wendlandii—36-inch rosette, 15-inch lush green foliage.

PHOENIX   date palm
Palmaceae 55-75F

Impressive palms with crowns of feathery leaves, these need little care. Grow in bright light; soak soil and then let dry out before watering again. From Africa and Asia where they reach 100 feet, indoors date palms stay medium height, about 6 feet. They like small pots, a 5-inch container is fine for a mature specimen, and although they are difficult to move, occasionally they do need a deep soaking in a tub. Propagate by seeds or buy young plants.

P. canariensis—shiny green feathery leaves.
P. dactylifera—the "date palm" with fine blue-green foliage.

P. roebelenii—dwarf to about 40 inches; most often seen with thick crowns of dark green leaves.

PHORMIUM   New-Zealand-flax
Liliaceae 50-70F

Lovely lance leaves margined red or orange make these excellent plants for a corner. In time, they grow tall, to 7 or 8 feet, but young ones do not exceed 4 feet. Give sun and let soil dry out between waterings. Dark red flowers, but they rarely appear indoors. Attractive terrace plants against a brick wall or redwood fence. New plants from offsets.

P. atropurpureum—green leaves delicately marked with bronze.
P. tenax—dark brownish-green leaves edged red; the most popular one.

PHYLLITIS   hart's-tongue fern
Polypodiaceae 50-65F

A 20-inch fern with dark green crinkly fronds, this thrives indoors if kept cool and makes a nice shapely plant. Grow in shade and give plenty of water; it will even tolerate the dim light of an entry hall for many months. Set in a decorative container to show off the flamboyant fronds. Propagate by division.

P. scolopendrium cristatum

Piggy-back-plant see TOLMIEA

PILEA   aluminum-plant
Urticaceae 50-75F

Small foliage plants with plain or variegated leaves and clusters of tiny flowers. Good ground-cover for planters or large pots. Keep soil moist. Propagate by cuttings.

* *P. cadierei*—to 12 inches or more, "aluminum-plant" or "watermelon pilea," silver-and-green foliage, rose-red flowers.
* *P. involucrata*—to 12 inches or more, bushy brown leaves and rose-red blooms.
* *P. microphylla*—"artillery plant," a tiny ground-cover.
* *P. nummulariaefolia*—to 8 inches, "creeping Charlie"; green with rose-red flowers, fine for baskets.

* *P. repens*—to 12 inches or more, quilted coppery-brown round leaves, greenish-white blooms.

Pincushion cactus see MAMMILLARIA and CACTUS

Pineapple see ANANAS and BROMELIADS

Pineapple-lily see EUCOMIS

Pink agapanthus see TULBAGHIA

Pink calla see ZANTEDESCHIA

PITTOSPORUM   *Pittosporaceae* 50-70F

Decorative evergreens to 40 inches with thick glossy green leaves. Likes slightly acid soil; grow in bright light or in shade and keep soil almost dry all year. A good tub plant, or better, train it to become a miniature tree. Propagate by cuttings.

P. Tobira—thick leathery green leaves; white or greenish-yellow flowers with orange-blossom scent.

variegatum—green-and-yellow foliage; needs more care.

PLATYCERIUM   staghorn fern
Polypodiaceae 60-80F

Extraordinary epiphytes with forked fronds; they do surprisingly well indoors. However, they must be grown on osmunda on slabs of decay-resistant wood (cedar or cork), soaked daily in a tub of water. The fertile fronds are pendent and give the plant the common name; the sterile ones are flat and rest against the shield of wood. Give plants strong light or semishade and mist them frequently; otherwise, they will not survive. Propagate from plantlets.

P. bifurcatum—grayish-green fronds to 3 feet.
P. grande—spreading glossy green fronds to 6 feet, for a plant room.

136

P. stemaria—curious thick gray-green fronds to 3 feet.

P. veitchii—vigorous, rounded basal fronds to 2 feet.

P. wilhelminae-reginae—superb, glossy green-silvery fronds to 3 feet.

PLECTRANTHUS   prostrate-coleus
Labiatae 60-75F

Foolproof plants with waxy green scalloped leaves on trailing stems and pretty little flowers on and off throughout the year. Allied to coleus, these plants are seldom seen but certainly are worth space at a window. Grow in light or shade and keep soil evenly moist. Propagate by seeds sown in spring or by cuttings at any time.

P. australis—to 20 inches, waxy saw-toothed leaves, pink flowers, for basket growing.

variegatum—irregular white edges.

P. coleoides—to 20 inches, small crinkled leaves, white-and-purple blooms.

P. oertendahlii—to 20 inches, apple-green foliage veined silver, pale pink flowers.

PLUMBAGO   leadwort
Plumbaginaceae 50-70F

Large bushy 36-inch shrubs with small leaves and cheerful flowers in summer, a sprawling climber if supported or it can trail. A mature specimen in bloom is a breathtaking sight. Give full sun and plenty of water during growth. Feed moderately; in winter carry almost dry.

58 *Plectranthus oertendahlii.* Merry Gardens photo

Mist foliage in summer. Propagate by seeds or cuttings.

P. capensis—2-inch phloxlike azure-blue flowers.
P. indica coccinea—1-inch scarlet blooms; rare, smaller plant than above.

Pocketbook-plant see CALCEOLARIA

PODOCARPUS Southern-yew
Podocarpaceae 55-75F

Evergreen shrubs and trees that make superb tub plants—one with slender growth to 6 feet, the other spreading. Grow in shade and let soil dry between waterings. New plants from seed.

P. macrophylla maki—erect branching waxy black-and-green leaves.
P. nagi—spreading shining green foliage.

Poet's jasmine see JASMINUM

Poinsettia see EUPHORBIA

Poison primrose see PRIMULA

POLYPODIUM polypody
Polypodiaceae 55-75F

Easy tropicals for an indoor planter or a sunroom. Robust, to 30 inches, with bold-textured blue-gray fronds and colorful orange-brown or white scaly rhizomes, irregular, sometimes an inch in diameter, and the reason for the common name. Grow in shallow tubs or hanging baskets in a mixture of humus, sphagnum, and sand. Keep moist and mist often. Give winter sun, shade in summer. Propagate by division in spring.

P. aureum glaucum—hare's-foot fern, blue-gray fronds.
  mandaianum—crested type.
P. polycarpon—yellow-green fronds.
P. subauriculatum—long pendent fronds, good for basket.

Polypody see POLYPODIUM

POLYSCIAS
Araliaceae 55-75F

Small heart-shaped leaves and compact growth make these fine plants, while young, for dish gardens and terrariums. They require north light and an evenly moist soil. Propagate by cuttings at any time.

P. balfouriana marginata—grayish-green leathery foliage.
P. guilfoylei victoriae—green-and-white feathery leaves.

POLYSTICHUM holly fern
Polypodiaceae 55-70F

A charming group of ferns, some large, some small. Many have feathery fronds; others stiff foliage. Leaves grow from a partly underground dark scale-covered crown. Keep soil moist and slightly acid. In warm weather, set plants outside in protected places for refreshing showers. Propagate by division in spring.

P. acrostichoides—"Christmas fern," attractive feathery fronds, medium size.
P. aculaetum—"hedge fern," heavy 24-inch fronds, medium size.
P. adiantiforme—"leather fern," bright green fronds, medium size.
P. tsus-simense—dwarf, low and compact, triangular fronds with a bright metallic sheen, good for terrariums.

Pomegranate see PUNICA

Poor-man's orchid see CYCLAMEN

PORTEA
Bromeliaceae 55-75F

Thirty-six-inch rosettes of dark green leaves and spectacular green-and-pink flower-heads in summer or fall make this a valued plant. It will grow in shade but does best in sun with osmunda kept moist. New plants from suckers.

P. Petropolitana extensa

Powder-puff cactus see MAMMILLARIA and CACTUS

Prayer-plant see MARANTA

Prickly-pear see OPUNTIA and CACTUS

Primrose see PRIMULA

PRIMULA   primrose
Primulaceae   45-55F

January-to-April-blooming gift plants for cool locations, these offer color during the darker months. Pick off flower buds to keep new flowers coming. Give filtered morning or afternoon sun and keep soil evenly moist; plants need a lot of water. If soil dries out, leaves turn yellow at the edges. A pinch of iron vitriol (at nurseries) and two drops of ammonia to a quart of water usually turn them green again. Pot up young plants that grow at the sides of the parent plant or sow seeds.

P. malacoides—to 26 inches, "fairy" or "baby primrose," tiny flowers, white through rose to red, encircle tall stems, look like a mist.
P. obconica—to 24 inches, "poison primrose," the large leaves irritate some sensitive skins; big clusters of white to red to purple flowers.
P. sinensis—to 24 inches, "Chinese primrose," lobed leaves; flowers in many shades.

Prostrate-coleus see PLECTRANTHUS

PTERIS   brake fern
Polypodiaceae   55-75F

Large and small ferns from the tropics with feathery growth, for table decoration or for the window garden. Give sun in winter, shade in summer. Keep soil evenly moist; 50 per cent humidity. Mist foliage frequently. Rapid growers under good conditions. New plants by division.

* P. cretica wilsonii—table fern, with slender 12-inch fronds.
P. ensiformis victoriae—"sword-brake," charming with variegated 12-inch fronds.
P. quadriaurita argyraea—white-and-green 24-inch fronds.
P. tremula—"Australian bracken," fast-growing yellow-green 24-inch fronds.

Punch-and-Judy orchid see GONGORA and ORCHIDS

PUNICA   pomegranate
Punicaceae   55-70F

Versatile treelike plants to 12 inches with shiny little green leaves and orange or red flowers; in autumn, brownish-red fruits. For window garden or bonsai training. Give full sun and let soil dry out between waterings; 50 per cent humidity. Leaves fall naturally in winter. Propagate by seeds.

P. granatum nana—with red flowers.
'Chico'—with orange flowers, does not bear fruit.

Pussy-ears see CYANOTIS

Queen-of-the-night see SELENICEREUS

Queensland umbrella-plant see SCHEFFLERA

Queen's-tears see BILLBERGIA

Queen's-wreath see PETREA

Rabbit's-foot fern see DAVALLIA and FERNS

Rainbow cactus see ECHINOCEREUS and CACTUS

Rainbow-flower see ACHIMENES and GESNERIADS

Rainbow-plant see CRYPTANTHUS

Rain-lily see ZEPHYRANTHES

REBUTIA   crown-cactus
Cactaceae   55-75F

Diminutive 1- to 5-inch barrel-shaped plants with bright flowers in spring. Grow in sun; these desert species require more water than most cacti except in winter when they can be grown cool (55F) and somewhat dry. Propagate by cuttings.

* R. kupperiana—tiny, with scarlet flowers.

* R. *minuscula*—flattened globe with white spines; scarlet blooms.
* R. *violaciflora*—depressed olive-green globe with purple flowers.

Red-pepper-plant see CAPSICUM

RECHSTEINERIA

Gesneriaceae 60-80F

Handsome South American plants with velvety green leaves and red, pink, or orange-red tubular flowers in summer. Plants need more light than African-violets, but don't grow them in strong sun; a west window is usually ideal. Water moderately and feed biweekly during growth; give 50 per cent humidity. After they bloom, leave the tubers in the pots and store them dry in a dim place (55F). After a three- to four-month rest, fresh growth will show; repot for the next season. New plants from seeds, cuttings, or tubers.

R. *cardinalis*—to 16 inches, dark green heart-shaped leaves and 2-inch brilliant red flowers.
R. *leucotricha*—"Brazilian edelweiss," to 14 inches, green leaves covered with hairs, 1-inch rose-coral flowers.
R. *lineata*—to 14 inches, hairy dark green leaves and small nodding dark red flowers in clusters of a dozen or more.
* R. *macropoda*—to 9 inches (often confused with R. *cyclophylla*), soft dark green heart-shaped leaves and brick-red flowers.
R. *verticillata* (*purpurea*)—"the double-decker plant," to 24 inches, pointed dark green leaves with serrated edges, hundreds of small wine-spotted pink flowers.

Resurrection plant see SELAGINELLA

RHAPHIDOPHORA   shingle-plant

Araceae 60-80F

A climber to 24 inches with dark, leathery foliage similar to that of monstera. Grow in sun or shade and keep soil evenly moist. Sponge leaves occasionally to keep them shiny. New plants from cuttings.

R. *celatocaulis*

RHAPIS   lady palm

Palmaceae 55-75F

Tough robust plants with fan fronds on tall cane stems. Grow at a north or west window and soak soil well, then allow to dry out before watering again. Provide an 8- or 10-inch container; repot only every three or four years. Propagate from suckers.

R. *excelsa*—to 5 feet, leathery glossy green leaves with 3 to 10 segments.
R. *humilis*—slender, more graceful and slightly smaller in size.

RHIPSALIS   chain or mistletoe cactus

Cactaceae 55-80F

Fine group of spineless generally epiphytic cacti with pendent growth to 36 inches and handsome colorful berries in winter, attractive for baskets. Pot in osmunda or fir bark or osmunda-soil mix and grow moist in summer, somewhat dry in winter; give plants bright light. New ones from cuttings.

R. *burchelli*—"mistletoe cactus," cream-colored flowers, pink berries.
R. *capilliformis*—cream-colored flowers, white berries.
R. *paradoxa*—three-angled stems, white flowers, red berries.

RHODODENDRON   azalea

Ericaceae 50-60F

Azaleas make outdoor gardens blaze with color and in the home they also make bright accents for bright windows. Mainly, they are seasonal gift plants—bushy or treelike to perhaps 20 inches—but it is not impossible to carry them through the years. (Whether or not the one you receive is a hardy type for the outdoor garden, it is difficult to discover; even the florist can rarely tell you.) Indoors, grow as cool as possible; mist foliage frequently, and keep soil evenly moist. To accomplish this, stand the pot in a deep bowl and pour in water every morning; it will be empty by night for azaleas require a great deal of moisture. (About once a week, skip the morning watering, let the soil get just a little dry, and stand the pot in a pail

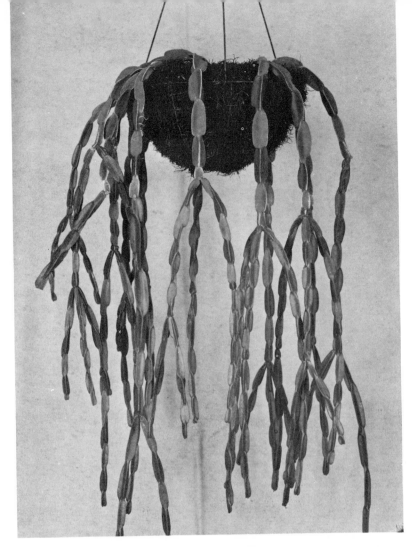

59 *Rhipsalis paradoxa.* Alberts & Merkel Bros., Inc. photo

with water to within an inch of the rim and let stay until top soil feels moist.) Depending on whether you received an in-bloom or simply well-budded plant, it will have color for weeks to months. Put an in-bud plant in the sun, and an in-bloom plant in a light place. After flowers fade, a slight rest is necessary so give your plant less water until weather is warm enough to take it outside. In May, repot in a fresh soil mixture and with plenty of humus, and set on a porch or sink the pot in the shaded garden. Water daily and fertilize about once a month. To encourage bud formation for next year, leave the plant outdoors until the temperature is likely to go below 40F. Then bring it in, admit plenty of fresh air during the first weeks indoors, and mist tops daily. It will need less water now than when in bloom and no fertilizing until November. Start weekly feedings then. Depending on type, budding will commence in early December or later. These are my favorites:

R. 'Alaska'—double white.
R. 'Beatrice'—double brick-red flowers.
R. 'Constance'—single cerise pink.
R. 'Coral Bells'—double pink with darker centers.
R. 'Hexe'—double red.
R. 'Orange Queen'—double pink-orange.
R. 'Pink Pearl'—double salmon-rose.
R. 'Purity'—double white.
R. 'Salmon Beauty'—semidouble salmon.
R. 'Snow'—double white.
R. 'Sweetheart'—double salmon-pink.

141

RHOEO   Moses-in-the-cradle
Commelinaceae 55-75F

Easy plants with fleshy olive-green lance leaves and little white flowers in dense umbels almost hidden by two boat-shaped bracts. Give bright light and constant moisture. New plants from seeds.

R. *discolor*—to 12 inches, rosette of stiff dark green almost black leaves, purple underneath.
    variegata—with white border.

RHYNCHOSTYLIS   fox-tail orchid
Orchidaceae 60-80F

Large 30-inch epiphytes with pendent scapes of small highly scented summer flowers, dozens to a scape, and long leathery dark green leaves in fountain growth. Pot in fir bark kept moist at all times—plants do not rest. Grow in full sun. New plants from specialists.

R. *gigantea*—great plumes of pink-and-white blooms.
R. *retusa*—long stems of 1-inch rose-colored flowers.

RIVINA   rouge-plant
Phytolaccaceae 55-70F

With oval leaves, drooping clusters of white flowers, and lustrous red berries on and off throughout the year, this 24-inch plant is very pretty at the window. Grow in sun with evenly moist soil. New plants from cuttings.

R. *humilis*

60 *Rivina humilis.* Merry Gardens photo

ROHDEA

Liliaceae 55-75F

A favorite 24-inch ornamental house plant in China and Japan, with stiff, dark handsome leaves forming a pleasing rosette; white flowers. Place in light and keep soil evenly moist. Slow-growing, this lives for years without much attention. Wipe foliage with damp cloth once a month or so to bring out the glowing foliage color. Decorative red berries usually produced in fall. Propagate by cuttings.

R. japonica—thick leathery dull green leaves.
    marginata—with white borders.

ROSA   rose

Rosaceae 50-60F

The miniatures make delightful house plants, perfect replicas of the standard roses. Grow in a sunny well-ventilated place with soil kept evenly moist and biweekly feedings, except in late fall and early winter. At that time cut back plants a little and store in a cool frostfree (about 40F) place. In January start forcing bloom with some warmth and plenty of water. Mist tops daily and watch foliage for red spider. Propagate by seeds or cuttings.

* 'Bo-Peep'—6 to 8 inches, double star-shaped pink flowers in clusters.
* 'Cinderella'—to 10 inches, single shell-pink to white.
* 'Lilac Time'—4 to 10 inches, floriferous, lavender clusters.
* 'Lollipop'—6 to 15 inches, brilliant red clusters.
* 'Pixie'—3 to 9 inches, single pure white.
* 'Tinker Bell'—5 to 10 inches, purple-red clusters.

RUELLIA

Acanthaceae 60-75F

Graceful, with dark green leaves and pale pink or red or white flowers from fall into spring. Grow in full sun and keep soil barely moist; they are sensitive to too much water. Good for basket or bracket, dependable and colorful in the window garden. New plants from cuttings.

R. amoena—to 24 inches, wavy oval leaves and red flowers.

R. macrantha—to 40 inches, dark green leaves and rose-colored blooms.
R. makoyana—to 18 inches, silver-veined leaves and carmine flowers.

Sago-plant see CYCAS

SAINTPAULIA   African-violet

Gesneriaceae 65-80F

From the original few African species, hybridists have created thousands of cultivars, free flowering and sturdy, much easier to grow. Foliage may be somewhat velvety or smooth, scalloped or wavy, lance or heart-shaped, green or variegated. Flowers are single, double, or semidouble in shades of pink, blue, lavender, purple, or white. Be sure to sterilize soil or use mixes packaged specifically for these plants. Set them so that the crown is slightly above the soil line. Give bright light in spring and summer, some sun in fall and winter, and always a good circulation of air. Water soil moderately to keep it slightly moist but never wet; apply only tepid water to soil or leaves; cold water spots foliage. Bottom watering (filling saucer with water) is often advised to insure even moisture at the roots but you can water from the top, too, and alternating the two methods is a good idea. In any case, arrange perfect drainage when you pot plants and don't let plants stand in water. Humidity of 40 to 60 per cent is essential and promoted by setting plants on pebble-filled trays. Dry air causes leaf curl and bud drop. Propagate by leaf cuttings or seeds. Here are some I enjoy:

S. 'Alakazam'—double lavender.
S. 'Big Boy Blue'—double blue.
S. 'Bloom Burst'—semidouble pink.
S. 'Chateaugay'—double blue-purple.
S. 'Cochise'—semidouble red star-shaped.
S. 'Flash'—double rose-pink.
S. 'Happy Time'—double pink.
* S. 'Honeyette'—miniature, reddish-lavender bicolor.
S. 'Lady Wilson'—double lavender-blue edged white.
S. 'Miniature White Girl'—single white flowers.
S. 'Purple Knight'—single dark purple.
* S. 'Pink Rock'—miniature, double pink.
S. 'Red Honey'—double red.

143

S. 'Spitfire'—single deep pink fringed white.

* S. 'Tinkle'—miniature, double lavender.

* S. 'White Doll'—miniature.

S. 'White Perfection'—immense double.

S. 'Zorro'—double lavender.

SANSEVIERIA   snake-plant
Liliaceae   55-75F

Indestructible, old-fashioned favorites with sharp-pointed thick fleshy leaves; some are upright, others form a ground-hugging rosette. Mottled and variegated forms thrive in sun or shade. Tolerant to moisture, the plants grow only if kept moist; kept dry they remain attractive but hardly change in size. Mature plants produce tall sprays of pretty fragrant pink-white flowers. Propagate by offsets.

S. *cylindrica*—to 60 inches, dark green arching leaves, several to a shoot.

S. *ehrenbergii*—to 18 inches, slow-growing, blue leaves edged white in fan fashion.

S. *parva*—to 18 inches, dense rosette of green leaves with dark crossbands.

S. *trifasciata laurentii*—to 30 inches, lance leaves with yellow bands.

Satinwood see MURRAEA

SAXIFRAGA   strawberry-geranium
Saxifragaceae   55-75F

With geranium-like leaves and strawberry coloring, these are charming trailing plants for dish gardens, terrariums, or window sills. Grow in 3- or 4-inch pots or in baskets; give bright light with less moisture and warmth in winter. Watch for mealy bugs. New plants from runners.

S. *sarmentosa*—to 20 inches, most common; coarsely-toothed reddish leaves veined white, white flowers.

'Tricolor'—to 18 inches, dark green, rosy-red-and-white foliage, a veritable rainbow.

Scarborough-lily see VALLOTA

SCHEFFLERA Queensland umbrella-plant
Araliaceae 55-75F

Tough tub plants to 60 inches with large decorative fronds and flowers in panicles. Give bright light and water only once or twice a week; neglect them and they still seem to thrive. Good for public rooms; well-grown specimens become handsome trees. New plants from seeds or cuttings of half-ripened stems.

S. actinophylla—fast growing with large palmate leaves and greenish flowers.

S. digitata—yellow hairy foliage, 7 to 10 leaflets, greenish-yellow flowers, needs cooler location.

SCHIZOCENTRON Spanish-shawl-plant
Melastomaceae 55-75F

For a sunny window, a fine creeping basket plant with dark green hairy leaves and pretty vivid purple flowers starting in late winter and continuing colorful into summer. Keep soil evenly moist. Propagate by cuttings.

S. elegans

62 *Schizocentron elegans.* Merry Gardens photo

SCHLUMBERGERA   Christmas cactus
Cactaceae 55-70F

Appealing jungle cacti to 24 inches with scalloped margined branches that distinguish them from the toothed *Zygocactus* varieties. With cascades of flowers in pink or red or salmon, they are an example of nature at her best. Give these epiphytes sun in fall and winter; keep soil barely moist then. In spring and summer, water plants freely. In mid-October or November, give plants 12 hours of uninterrupted darkness and cool nights (55F) so they will set buds. Humidity, 60 per cent. A mature specimen is an impressive sight. Propagate by cuttings.

S. bridgesii—the old-fashioned "Christmas cactus," red blooms.
'Pink Perfection'—bright clear color, large flowers.
'Parna'—small bright red blooms.
'Salmonea'—scarlet flowers.

Scilla see CHAPTER 5

SCINDAPSUS (POTHOS)   ivy-arum
Araceae 55-75F

Climbers to 36 inches, with smooth dark green leaves splashed with yellow, white, or silver; all amenable vines even for apartments. Grow in a light well-ventilated place but avoid drafts; keep soil evenly moist. Nice for basket or bracket. Propagate by cuttings.

S. aureus—12-inch dark green leaves laced with yellow.
'Marble Queen'—green leaves richly streaked white.
'Orange Queen'—apricot-and-yellow foliage.
'Silver Moon'—creamy yellow foliage.
S. pictus argyraeus—6-inch satiny green leaves edged silver.

Screw-pine see PANDANUS

Sea-urchin cactus see ECHINOPSIS and CACTUS

SEDUM   stonecrop
Crassulaceae 50-70F

Most of these succulents are low-growing with thick or needle, blue or green leaves; many uses for indoor gardens. Some have bushy growth, others form low mats, and some trail. All need full sun with soil dried out between waterings. Try them for dish gardens. New plants from seed sown in spring.

* *S. adolphii*—to 6 inches, yellow-green bushy type, white flowers in spring.
* *S. dasyphyllum*—to 2 inches, blue-green mats, pink flowers in summer.
* *S. lineare*—to 6 inches, trailing, needle leaves, yellow blooms in summer.
S. morganianum—to 36 inches "burro tail," trailing, blue-green foliage, yellow blooms in summer.
* *S. multiceps*—to 4 inches, shrubby with yellow flowers in summer.

SELAGINELLA   club-moss
Selaginellaceae 55-75F

Small ferny plants, excellent for terrariums and dish gardens. Some are attractive hanging plants, others are creepers good for covering the soil of larger plants. Grow in shade; soak soil and let dry out between waterings; 50 per cent humidity. Avoid water on foliage; it causes rot. Propagate by cuttings.

S. kraussiana—12-inch creeper with tiny bright green leaves.
* *S. lepidophylla*—6-inch ball, the "resurrection plant"; a dense mat when dry; it only needs soaking to live again.
S. martensii variegata—to 12 inches, upright with lacy silver-tipped foliage.
S. uncinata—to 24 inches, creeper with blue-green leaves.
* *S. willdenovii*—to 10 inches, nice climber with blue-green leaves.

SELENICEREUS   night-blooming-cereus
Cactaceae 55-75F

Climbing to 7 feet, generally epiphytic and bearing exquisite fragrant summer flowers, these plants can be tied to a bark support to grow tall

XIII A COLORFUL QUARTET. (Upper left) Egyptian star-flowers, Pentas, fine for winter bloom. (Upper right) *Smithiantha*, a gesneriad. *Park Seed Co. photos* (Lower left) Kohleria, 'Rongo'. *Robert Wright, Jr. photo for Gesneriad Saintpaulia News* (Lower right) An exquisite basket fuchsia grown by the author. *Joyce Wilson photo*

XIV   TWO COLLECTIONS. (Above) Five foliage plants: Ferns, a tall arrow-leaved alocasia, the 'Iron Cross' begonia, and a tradescantia. (Below) Six sturdy bromeliads: *Aechmea fasciata, Vriesea splendens,* and *A. chantinii* in the back row; *Guzmania magnifica,* a cryptanthus species, and a neoregelia in the foreground. *Fennell Orchid Co. photos*

XV   SOME HANDSOME CACTI. (Upper left) The spectacular night-blooming cereus, *Selenicereus Donkelaari*. (Upper right) Wooly Torch, *Cephalocereus palmeri*, an unusual cactus. (Lower left) An orchid cactus, *Epiphyllum*, in bloom in May. (Lower right) Living-rock cactus from Mexico, *Ariocarpus furfuraceus*. *Johnson Cactus Gardens photos*

XVI **PLANTS WITH GRACE.** (Above) A cascading tuberous begonia, beautiful basket plant. *Brown Bulb Ranch photo* (Below) Kalanchoe 'Jingle Bells', a succulent with pendent blooms. *Park Seed Co. photo*

or allowed to hang. They are too large for a window but suitable for plant room or sun porch. Provide a sandy soil and 5- or 6-inch pots; I use pound coffee cans painted. Plants need sun in winter, shade in summer. Water moderately in fall and winter, flood the rest of the year; 30 to 50 per cent humidity. Get your camera ready when they bloom; no one will believe the dinner-plate size of these beauties. Propagate by cuttings or buy young plants from a specialist.

S. *donkelaari*—7-inch white flowers.
S. *grandiflorus*—"queen-of-the-night," 7-inch white or salmon-pink flowers.
S. *macdonaldiae*—12-inch gold-and-white blooms.
S. *pteranthus*—12-inch white blooms.

SEMPERVIVUM houseleek
Crassulaceae 50-70F

Stemless, many-leaved rosettes, half-inch to 12 inches across with offsets from leaf axils. Plants soon become decorative colorful mats. Starry white, yellow, or pink flowers in dense heads open in summer, then the flowering rosettes die but are replaced by new ones. Easy to grow, plants need morning or afternoon sun and moderately moist soil. Nice for dish gardens. New plants from offsets.

* S. *arachnoideum*—the "cobweb houseleek," to 4 inches, with white hairs, red blooms.
* S. *montanum*—to 6 inches, clusters of pointed fleshy green leaves, purple flowers.
* S. *tectorum calcareum*—to 12 inches, "hen-and-chickens," leathery light green foliage, pink blooms.

SENECIO cineraria
Compositae 50-70F

These florist plants bloom for two to three weeks at Easter, with round heads of daisy flowers in vivid colors. Place in a bright not sunny spot, as cool as possible, and water heavily. Best treated as an annual to be grown each year from seed, or buy new plants.

S. *confusus*—vining type, orange or orange-red flowers.

S. *cruentus*—florist upright type to 20 inches, white, pink, or purple flowers.

Senna see CASSIA

Sentry palm see HOWEIA

Seven stars see ARIOCARPUS

Shingle-plant see RHAPHIDOPHORA

Shooting-star see CYCLAMEN

Shower-tree see CASSIA

Shrimp-plant see BELOPERONE

Silk-oak see GREVILLEA

SINNINGIA gloxinia
Gesneriaceae 60-75F

Glamorous plants from tropical Brazilian forests with single or double tubular or slipper flowers in bright colors. While the species are dormant in winter, today's hybrids bloom at intervals throughout the year. Tubers from mail-order suppliers can be started in spring or fall. Put one to a 5-inch pot in equal parts of sand, loam, and peatmoss. Set the tuber, hollow side up, and cover with soil. Keep evenly moist in a warm place (about 60F) with 50 per cent humidity. When flowers fade, gradually decrease watering. Remove tops and store tubers in pots in a cool dark place. Keep soil barely moist, rest from 6 to 10 weeks (no more) or tubers will lose vitality. Repot in fresh soil in a larger pot. Propagate from tip cuttings.

S. *barbata*—4- to 6-inch blue-green leaves, white flowers streaked red.
S. *concinna*—about 2 inches, small tubular lavender flowers with white throats.
* S. *pusilla*—2 inches across, perhaps the tiniest house plant, single pale lavender tubular flowers.
'Dollbaby'—3 inches across, single tubular lavender blooms.
S. *regina*—to 10 inches, velvety dark green

147

leaves with white veins, 2-inch tubular dark purple slipper flowers.

S. speciosa—to 12 inches, ovate green leaves, nodding pink or blue slipper flowers.

SMITHIANTHA   temple-bells
Gesneriaceae 65-80F

Handsome richly-colored foliage plants with splendid bell-shaped flowers from November through May. In March or April, start each rhizome in a 4- or 5-inch pot, planting 1 inch deep. Grow at an east or south window; keep soil evenly moist, humidity from 60 to 70 per cent. After plants bloom, store rhizomes dry in the pots in a cool shaded place for about three months. Then repot and return to a bright window. Propagate from seeds or division of rhizomes.

S. cinnabarina—to 16 inches, serrated leaves with a covering of red hairs, orange-red flowers.

S. multiflora—to 20 inches, deep green foliage, creamy unspotted flowers.

S. zebrina—to 30 inches, rounded dark green leaves marked brown or purple, covered with silvery hairs, bright red flowers spotted darker.

Cornell Series Hybrids
S. 'Abbey'—peach
S. 'Carmel'—red
S. 'Cloisters'—apricot
S. 'San Gabriel'—straw-yellow

63 *Smithiantha.* Merry Gardens photo

Snake-plant see SANSEVIERIA

SOLANUM Jerusalem-cherry
Solanaceae 50-60F

Small dark-leaved shrubs from Brazil and Uruguay, the one with orange-red fruits in winter is known as the Jerusalem-cherry, a favorite Christmas gift plant; the other is prized for fragrant star-shaped flowers. Plants need bright light and soil kept barely moist. In winter, grow cool, about 50F, with little moisture. If you want to hold over from year to year, set them out in the garden in late spring and prune back to about 10 inches. Propagate by seeds.

S. jasminoides—to 6 feet, shrubby climber with scented white flowers, in fall or winter.
S. pseudo-capsicum—to 3 feet, "Jerusalem cherry," upright with white flowers and red or yellow fruit, in fall and winter.

Southern-yew see PODOCARPUS

Spanish-shawl-plant see SCHIZOCENTRON

SPARAXIS wand-flower
Iridaceae 50-70F

These bulbs with narrow leaves and arching flower stems make lovely 20-inch pot plants. The 2-inch flowers appear in April and May. In fall, set 5 or 6 bulbs 1 inch deep in a 6-inch pot; at first water moderately. As growth develops, water freely. Place in sun with night temperature not more than 55F or flowers will blast. When bloom is over, dry off foliage gradually; then store plants in their pots absolutely dry. Repot in fresh soil in fall. Propagate by division or offsets.

S. grandiflora—flowers yellow or purple.
S. tricolor—multicolored blooms.

SPARMANNIA indoor linden
Tiliaceae 55-70F

Evergreen with pale hairy leaves and charming white flowers in winter and spring. Good window plants that need bright light and plenty of water; 40 per cent humidity. Set outside in summer. Can grow to 10 feet; prune occasionally to keep to 40 inches. New plants from tip cuttings in spring.

S. africana—umbels of single white flowers.
flore-pleno—double flowers.

SPATHIPHYLLUM
Araceae 55-75F

Twenty-inch aroids from South America with shiny leaves and white spathe flowers resembling anthuriums. Bloom usually appears in winter but sometimes in summer or fall. Give plants a bright location and keep soil evenly moist except in winter; then grow on the dry side. Propagate by seeds.

S. clevelandii—long leaves and white flowers.
S. floribundum—dwarf to 14-inches, green leaves and white flowers.

Spider-plant see CHLOROPHYTUM

Spider-orchid see ANSELLIA and ORCHIDS

Spiderwort see TRADESCANTIA

Spiral ginger see COSTUS

SPREKELIA Jacobean-lily
Amaryllidaceae 55-70F

A fine 20-inch bulbous pot plant with spectacular red flowers in June before foliage develops. Pot one bulb to a 6-inch container in late winter or spring. Set in a sunny place and keep soil evenly moist from time growth starts until September; then carry somewhat dry until December; 70 per cent humidity. Propagate by offsets at potting time.

S. formosissima

Staghorn fern see PLATYCERIUM and FERNS

STANHOPEA
Orchidaceae 60-80F

Warm-preference orchids with 30-inch leaves and large late-summer spikes borne from the base of the bulb. Flowers in scapes are very fragrant and of vibrant color but last only a few days. Grow these epiphytes in osmunda in slatted redwood baskets; give plenty of water all year, sun in winter and spring, some shade in summer and fall; 70 per cent humidity. New plants from a specialist.

S. *insignis*—one to four 4-inch pale yellow flowers spotted purple.
S. *oculata*—three to seven 6-inch flowers, usually yellow with orange.
S. *wardii*—three to seven 8-inch flowers, usually white with purple spots.

STAPELIA   carrion-flower
Asclepiadaceae 55-75F

Succulents from South Africa, star-shaped and five-petaled, usually with evil-smelling flowers. Plants grow well in a sunny window; soak soil and then let dry a little between waterings. Grow almost dry in winter. Not my idea of a good house plant but children are fascinated by the unusual shape. New ones from division of clumps.

S. *hirsuta*—to 12 inches, hairy brownish flowers.
* S. *variegata*—to 6 inches, the "star-flower"; greenish-yellow with brown spots.

Star cactus see ASTROPHYTUM and CACTUS

Star-flower see STAPELIA

Star-jasmine see TRACHELOSPERMUM

Star-of-Bethlehem see CAMPANULA and ORNITHOGALUM

Starplant see CRYPTANTHUS and BROMELIADS

STEPHANOTIS   Madagascar-jasmine
Asclepiadaceae 50-70F

Scented waxy-white flowers in June, July, and August cover this vine, a handsome foil for the dark green leathery leaves. Plants thrive in an east or south window with 30 to 50 per cent humidity. Mist frequently to keep in health. Water soil about three times a week except in winter when once a week is enough. Can grow to 15 feet but my plant on a trellis in a pot has

never exceeded 30 inches. Propagate by cuttings in spring.

S. *floribunda*

Stepladder plant see COSTUS

Stonecrop see SEDUM

Strawberry-geranium see SAXIFRAGA

STRELITZIA   bird-of-paradise
Musaceae 55-75F

Large tropical plants with banana-like leaves and exotic flowers that resemble birds. Give plants a sunny place and plenty of water except in winter when they can be grown somewhat dry and cooler (60F). Only mature specimens with seven to ten leaves bloom. Essentially these are terrace plants for summer flowers, but I have also seen them in glorious color indoors. These are a favorite of flower arrangers. Propagate by division of tubers or sow seeds.

S. *nicolai*—to 4 feet or more, less showy blooms, white and purple.
S. *reginae*—slow-growing to 6 feet, most popular with orange-and-purple flowers.

STREPTOCARPUS   cape-primrose
Gesneriaceae 50-75F

Under-rated gesneriads with rich green leaves and funnel-shaped flowers from pure white through pink, rose, salmon, blue, and deep violet. Place in bright light or sun and keep soil evenly moist; feed moderately in growth. Different species rest at different times so watch for a period of dormancy and don't try to force plants then. Stop fertilizing and water only to prevent wilting. After a few months, fresh leaves will appear; then repot. Propagate by seeds or cuttings.

S. *dunnii*—generally one large leaf, red flowers.
S. *grandis*—curious stemless plant with but one large leaf to 36 inches long, small blue flowers.
S. *rexii*—leaves to 8 inches long, blue or white flowers.
S. *saxorum*—trailer to 16 inches with succulent leaves and 1½-inch lavendar flowers.

String-of-hearts see CEROPEGIA

Surinam-cherry see EUGENIA

STROBILANTHES *Acanthaceae* 50-75F

Attractive house plants, to about 2 feet, not often seen but quite decorative for a sunny place. One bears pale purple flowers that look like foxgloves, the other is valued for its handsome blue foliage tinged with silver as well as for bloom. Keep soil wet but not soggy; 30 to 50 per cent humidity. Only good for one season so take cuttings in spring for new plants.

S. dyerianus—8-inch purple-green leaves; violet flowers.
S. isophyllus—4-inch willowy toothed leaves, pinkish or blue-and-white flowers.

SWAINSONA
Leguminosae 50-60F

White or red flowers like sweet peas and lacy light green foliage on a 3- to 4-foot semiclimbing plant. Grow in sun; water heavily until September and then keep soil only fairly moist. Prune after blooming; stake plants. Provide 30 to 50 per cent humidity and pinch young shoots when they are a few inches tall. Mist foliage frequently. New plants from seed.

S. albiflora—pure white.
S. galegifolia—to 3 feet with red blooms.
S. violacea—rose-colored blooms.

64 *Strobilanthes dyerianus.* Merry Gardens photo

Sweet olive see OSMANTHUS

Swiss-cheese-plant see MONSTERA

Sword-brake see PTERIS

Sword fern see NEPHROLEPIS and FERNS

SYNGONIUM arrowhead *Araceae* 55-75F

Desirable old-fashioned pot plants to 30 inches with green or variegated foliage, small or large, lance or arrow-shaped. Fast growing and easy in bright light or shade, in soil or in water. Propagate by cuttings.

S. podophyllum—trailer with 6-inch leaves.
    'Emerald Gem'—smaller rich green leaves.
    'Imperial White'—greenish-white foliage.
S. wendlendii—dainty creeper with dark green leaves with white veins.

Taro see COLOCASIA

Teddy-bear plant see CYANOTIS

Temple-bells see SMITHIANTHA and GESNERIADS

Thanksgiving cactus see ZYGOCACTUS and CACTUS

TOLMIEA piggy-back-plant
Saxifragaceae 55-70F

A creeper that bears new plants on the back of old leaves. With fresh green toothed leaves, it spreads to about 30 inches. Give sun or full light and keep soil moist. Grows almost untended. Propagate by plantlets.

T. menziesii

THUNBERGIA black-eyed-Susan-vine
Acanthaceae 50-70F

Uncommonly beautiful plants with funnelform cheerful flowers and attractive foliage. Grow in full sun, the soil kept evenly moist except in winter when plants can be almost dry. Train most of them to a pot trellis; they stay quite small indoors. *T. erecta* is best as a tub plant for terrace. Propagate by seeds.

T. alata—to 6 feet, dark-centered yellow-orange or white summer flowers. Vine.
T. erecta—to 6 feet, dark green foliage, blue summer blooms.
T. grandiflora—to 5 feet, the "clock vine," large pale blue flowers in fall.

Tiger orchid see ODONTOGLOSSUM and ORCHIDS

Ti-plant see CORDYLINE

TILLANDSIA
Bromeliaceae 55-75F

Plants with tufted growth or palmlike foliage, they require full sun. Some are small, attractive for dish gardens or terrariums, others are large for the window. Pot in osmunda and keep moist. New plants from offsets.

T. cyanea—to 30 inches, dark green palm leaves and purple butterfly flowers in fall.
* *T. ionanthe*—to 3 inches, tufted beauty with red-and-violet blooms in summer.
T. juncea—to 12 inches, yellow-and-red inflorescence in summer.

TRACHELOSPERMUM star-jasmine
Apocynaceae 50-60F

A twining woody vine with glossy green foliage and fragrant white or yellow star-shaped flowers from early spring into fall. Prune plant to desired size; grows easily on a trellis. Give sun and keep soil moist. Plant stops growing at temperatures below 50F but in this semi-dormant state, budding is often initiated. Propagate by cuttings in spring.

T. jasminoides

TRADESCANTIA spiderwort, inchplant
Commelinaceae 55-75F

Fast-growing, small, trailing plants to 24 inches with oval fleshy leaves in cream, pink, red, mauve, gold, and dark green. Grow in shade or sun and in soil that dries out a little between waterings. Decorative in vase, basket, or pot. New plants from cuttings.

T. blossfeldiana—green foliage with silver hairs, pale purple flowers.

variegata—green-and-cream leaves.

T. *fluminensis*—"wandering jew," green leaves, white flowers.

    albo-vittata—blue-green-and-white foliage, white flowers.

T. *laekenensis*—green-and-pink foliage, white flowers.

* T. *multiflora*—miniature, dark green leaves, white flowers.

T. *navicularis*—"chain-plant," green leaves, boat-shaped coppery-green leaves, clusters of rosy-purple flowers.

Tree fern see BLECHNUM and FERNS

TULBAGHIA
Liliaceae 45-60F

Wonderful lilies on 20-inch stems for growing indoors; pale pink-to-lavender flowers and evergreen strap leaves. Arrange several corms 1-inch apart and half-an-inch deep in a 6-inch pot of sandy soil with a little peatmoss. Give plenty of water and feed bimonthly. In summer keep in shade, full sun the rest of the year. Blooms appear on and off from March to November. Propagate by offsets or seeds.

T. *cepacea (fragrans)*—the "pink agapanthus," umbels of scented flowers, foliage without garlic odor.

T. *violacea*—taller than above with pale lilac-colored blooms, foliage with garlic odor.

Tulips see CHAPTER 5

Umbrella-plant see CYPERUS

VALLOTA Scarborough-lily
Amaryllidaceae 50-65F

A large bulbous plant to 24 inches from South America with clusters of startling funnelform red flowers in summer and autumn, perfect accent for a cool place. In spring or fall, place a bulb in a rather small pot (4- or 5-inch); crowded roots induce good bloom. Be sure the point of the bulb is just below the surface of the soil. Grow in an east or south window; keep soil moderately moist except after flowering, then grow not quite so wet for about a month, but never dry out completely. Feed every 3 to

4 weeks during growth. New plants by offsets at potting time.

V. *speciosa*

VANDA
Orchidaceae 60-80F

These orchids that made Hawaii famous are not native but come from the Far East, the East Indies, and various other warm areas. Durable plants with succulent strap leaves, they produce tall wands of flat flowers, some 5 inches across. Plant these epiphytes in fir bark in 6- or 7-inch pots and do not disturb for several years. Keep bark moist, give full sun, and up to 80 per cent humidity. New plants from offsets ("kikis").

V. *caerulea*—to 30 inches, the "blue orchid," blue flowers in fall.

V. *roxburghii*—to 26 inches; pale green, purple, and brown flowers in summer, sometimes in spring, too.

V. *tricolor*—to 30 inches, generally yellow-to-pink flowers at various times of year.

VELTHEIMIA
Liliaceae 50-70F

A prettier house plant is hard to find; it usually blooms at Christmas with yellow-green to rose-tinged flowers on 20-inch stalks. Leaves are large, glossy green, and wavy margined. Place 2 or 3 bulbs in a 6-inch container with tips above the soil line. Grow in sun; keep soil moist except in summer when a dry rest of 3 to 5 weeks is needed. New plants from division of bulbs.

V. *viridifolia*

Velvet-plant see GYNURA

Violet-stemmed tara see XANTHOSOMA

Volcano-plant see BROMELIA and BROMELIADS

VRIESIA flaming-sword-plant
Bromeliaceae 55-75F

Feathery colorful plumes that last for several months make these ideal north-window plants.

Some kinds have pale green leaves, others dark green foliage marked and banded in brown; all have rosette growth. Pot in equal parts of osmunda and soil (these are terrestrials), and keep "vase" filled with water. Don't fertilize or spray with insecticides. Good plants for room-dividers. New plants from specialists.

V. carinata—to 18 inches, "lobster claws," smooth pale green leaves, yellow-and-crimson "sword."
V. hieroglyphica—to 30 inches, green-banded rosette with darker markings, tall yellow spikes of bloom.
V. malzinei—to 12 inches, plain green leaves, cylindrical orange spike.
V. splendens—to 20 inches, green foliage with mahogany stripes, orange "swords" on erect stems; does not produce offsets; but new plants push up from center of mature growth.

Wandering jew see TRADESCANTIA and ZEBRINA

Wand-flower see SPARAXIS

Watermelon pilea see PILEA

Waxplant see HOYA

WEDELIA

Compositae 50-70F

Yellow annual daisies bring summer to the window. Good trailing basket plant with 3-inch oblong fresh green leaves. Grow in sun and keep soil moist. Fast growing. Propagate by cuttings in spring or summer or from seeds.

W. trilobata

Weeping fig see FICUS

Willow-leaved jessamine see CESTRUM

Wireplant see MUEHLENBECKIA

Wood-sorrel see OXALIS

WOODWARDIA　chain fern
Polypodiaceae 55-75F

Not usually thought of for indoor growing, these stiff and leathery broad-frond-plants are a pleasing contrast to more delicate and airy types. Grow in bright light and keep soil barely moist, not wet; 30 to 50 per cent humidity. Give deep soaking in sink once a week. Set plants outdoors in summer where they benefit from warm rains. Usually large, to 30 inches across, you would not want more than one of these in your home. New plants by division.

W. fimbriata—leathery broad massive fronds.
W. orientalis—long drooping stiff fronds; good basket plant.

Yellow ginger see HEDYCHIUM

Yesterday-today-and-tomorrow see BRUNFELSIA

XANTHOSOMA

Araceae 65-85F

Jungle plants to 36 inches from South America with exquisite foliage; handsome for accent. They need bright light, an evenly moist soil, and 70 per cent humidity. New plants by division of underground tubers in summer.

X. lindenii 'Magnificum'—green-and-white 12-inch leaves.
X. violaceum—deep green foliage with purple edges, the "violet-stemmed tara."

ZANTEDESCHIA　calla-lily
Araceae 50-70F

With stunning funnel flowers on erect stalks, these are colorful additions to the winter indoor garden. Or start tubers in fall for summer bloom. Plant 1 bulb to a 4- or 5-inch pot in a mixture of peatmoss and sand. Supply larger containers when plants become potbound, not before. Place in a sunny window. Water moderately at first; when growth appears, keep soil fairly wet. Give liquid plant food once a month. After they flower, allow bulbs to ripen off naturally by gradually decreasing water. Then rest them in pots in a shaded cool spot and withhold water entirely. About August, take up bulbs and clean them; repot in fresh soil. Watch plants for red spider mites; spray with Kalthane. New plants from tiny offshoots or tubers.

Z. *aethiopica*—to 30 inches, the common calla, white flowers.

Z. *albo-maculata*—to 20 inches, spotted leaves and creamy white flowers.

Z. *elliottiana*—to 30 inches, the "golden calla," vivid yellow blooms.

Z. *rehmannii*—to 18 inches, the "pink calla," best for indoors.

Zebra-plant see APHELANDRA

ZEBRINA

Commelinaceae 55-75F

From Mexico, these pretty trailing silver-and-purple-leaved plants bear tiny purple flowers in spring and summer. Fast-growing, a basket specimen is a mass of color in sun or bright light. Keep soil evenly moist, or grow in a vase of water. Resembles tradescantia. Propagate by rooting cuttings.

Z. *pendula*—to 16 inches, "wandering jew," purple leaves with silver bands.

> *discolor*—to 16 inches, brown leaves with purple and silver stripes.
> * *minima*—to 12 inches, hairy purple-red foliage with silver bands.
> *quadricolor*—to 16 inches, purple-green leaves banded white and striped pink and purple.

ZEPHYRANTHES   rain-lily
Amaryllidaceae 50-70F

Small 8- to 14-inch summer-through-fall blooming bulbs with grassy foliage and pretty flowers —pink or white or orange. Some bloom at night, others in the day. In spring, pot 4 or 5

65   *Zebrina pendula quadricolor.* Merry Gardens photo

bulbs to a 6-inch pot; grow in a sunny window and let soil dry out between waterings. In winter, store bulbs dry in pots in a cool shaded place.

Z. *atamasco*—day-blooming, 3-inch white flowers.

Z. *grandiflora*—day-blooming, rose-pink flowers.

Z. *pedunculata*—white evening flowers partly open through day.

ZINGIBER   ginger

Zingiberaceae   60-80F

This commercial ginger requires little care. With reed growth to 30 inches, it has glossy dark grassy leaves and white flowers in summer. Grow it in sun or shade with soil kept moderately moist. New plants by division.

Z. *officinale*

ZYGOCACTUS   Thanksgiving or crab cactus

Cactaceae   50-70F

These popular plants from Brazil bring color to the fall indoor garden. With toothed branches that distinguish them from the scalloped *Schlumbergera* varieties, they bear exquisite, dainty blossoms from late October into December. In general, epiphytic, these 24- to 30-inch plants need sun in fall and winter, and bright light in spring and summer. Keep soil moderately moist except in fall when roots should be somewhat dry and plants grown quite cold (50F) *with 12 hours of uninterrupted darkness for a month to encourage bud formation.* Fifty per cent humidity. Pieces of stem root easily.

Z. 'Amelia Manda'—large crimson flowers.
Z. 'Gertrude W. Beahm'—bright red blooms.
Z. 'Llewellyn'—orange flowers.
Z. 'Orange Glory'—pale orange with white throat.
Z. 'Symphony'—delicate shade of orange, petals white at the base.

ZYGOPETALUM

Orchidaceae   50-75F

Mostly epiphytic orchids from different parts of the world, these have glossy green leaves and spikes of vivid fragrant flowers in shades of green, blue, and purple. The majority are winter blooming. Plant in 6- to 8-inch pots of osmunda and keep moderately moist in an airy bright location. When growth stops in fall (as leaves are fully expanded), rest plants without water and only an occasional misting; 50 per cent humidity. Sometimes leaves get black streaks and are unsightly but plants are not unhealthy; no remedy for discoloration at present. New plants from specialists.

Z. *crinitum*—to 26 inches, 2- to 3-inch green and violet-blue flowers in winter, several to a scape.
Z. *mackayi*—to 36 inches, 3- to 4-inch green, purple-brown and violet-blue flowers in winter, many to a scape.

Appendix

Kitchen Plants

Fruits and vegetables from the kitchen are fun for the indoor gardener. There is no cost, hardly any work, and lots of satisfaction. An avocado seed produces glossy green leaves in a short time, and a sweet potato becomes an attractive vine in a few weeks. Even the top of a pineapple, rooted, grows into a fine house plant. Carrot and beet tops develop decorative foliage; so do parsnip and horseradish.

Avocado. Place an avocado seed (pit), small end up, in a glass jar of water with the base *just touching the water*. You can suspend it with toothpicks. Set it in a bright window and change the water occasionally. When roots and first leaves form, plant in sandy soil in a 5-inch pot. Keep the soil quite wet. Don't discard the plant when it becomes leggy, but take off the lowest leaves, insert a bamboo stake in the soil for support, and grow your avocado into a handsome tree.

Sweet potato. Suspend a sweet potato with toothpicks in a glass jar of water (Don't use kiln-dried potatoes for this). Replenish water as it evaporates so the base of the potato is always immersed. Place in a sunny window; in a few weeks, pale green scalloped leaves appear. Train the plant to a small trellis or support, or grow it as a vine on strings around a window-frame.

Pineapple. Cut off the leafy top with a small section of the fruit and scoop out the pulp. Plant the top in a 4-inch pot of sandy soil and keep moist. Grow in sun.

Carrot, beet, parsnip, horseradish. Cut off the upper 2 inches of the tops and stand the cut pieces in water and pebbles in a bowl. Don't let the water cover the cut-off tops. Set in a bright window. Delicate fernlike foliage will sprout from the carrot; glossy green, almost red, leaves from the beet; fresh green foliage from parsnips and horseradish.

Citrus. Lemon or orange seeds germinate in pots of sandy soil at 70F. When young plants have growth, transfer them to small pots of rich loamy soil and place in a bright window.

Plants for Flowers Through the Year

Flowering plants are always a cheerful sight, and with only a dozen of them you can have color at the window throughout the year. Particularly welcome are those that bloom in winter when there is little outdoor color. Most of these are small (10 to 16 inches) or medium sized (16 to 26 inches) and so do not need much space, yet they will give dramatic accent among foliage plants indoors. The large plants (26 inches and above) are fine if you have room for one or more of them.

BOTANICAL NAME	COMMON NAME	SIZE	TIME OF BLOOM
Abutilon	flowering-maple	medium	February-March
Aechmea fasciata	living-vase	medium	March-May
Begonia semperflorens	wax begonias	small	almost everblooming
Beloperone guttata	shrimp-plant	medium	October-November
Bougainvillea	paper-flower	large	May-August
Capsicum annuum	red-pepper-plant	small	November
Columnea hirta		medium	April-July
Crossandra infundibuliformis		small	April-August
Dipladenia amoena	love-plant	large	June-July
Eranthemum nervosum	blue-sage	small	November-March
Jacobinia carnea		medium	April
Kalanchoe blossfeldiana		medium	December
Lycaste aromatica	cinnamon orchid	medium	October-November
Pentas lanceolata	star-flower	medium	September-January
Plumbago capensis		large	July-August
Punica granatum	pomegranate	small	October-November
Ruellia macrantha		medium	November-January
Sprekelia formosissima	Aztec-lily	medium	April
Tibouchina semidecandra		medium	May-September
Vriesea splendens	flaming-sword	small	June-August

Foliage Plants

Araucaria excelsa—Norfolk-Island-pine
Asplenium nidus—bird's-nest fern
Cordyline terminalis bicolor—ti-plant
Dieffenbachia amoena
Dizygotheca elegantissima—false aralia
Dracaena massangeana—cornplant
Ficus lyrata—fiddle-leaf fig

158

Hoffmannia roezlii
Maranta leuconeura kerchoveana—prayer-plant
Monstera deliciosa—Swiss-cheese-plant
Philodendron wendlandii
Schefflera actinophylla—umbrella-plant

Fragrant Plants

Citrus—lemon, lime, orange, grapefruit
Clerodendrum thomsoniae—glory-bower
Eucharis grandiflora—Amazon-lily
Hoya carnosa—waxplant
Hyacinthus—Dutch and French-Roman hyacinths
Jasinum officinale grandiflorum—poet's jasmine
Lycaste aromatica—cinnamon orchid
Narcissus—paperwhite narcissus
Osmanthus fragrans—sweet olive
Stephanotis floribunda—Madagascar-jasmine
Tulbaghia cepacea fragrans—pink agapanthus

Plant Societies and their Periodicals for Indoor Gardeners

African Violet Society of America   *African Violet Magazine*
P.O. Box 1326
Knoxville, Tenn. 37901

American Begonia Society   *The Begonian*
Mrs. Daisy Austin
1510 Kimberly Avenue
Anaheim, Calif. 92802

American Camellia Society   *American Camellia Journal*
Joseph H. Pyron
P.O. Box C
Tifton, Ga.

American Gloxinian Society   *The Gloxinian and the Other Gesneriads*
Mrs. Diantha Buell
Eastford, Conn. 06242

American Orchid Society   *American Orchid Society Bulletin*
Botanical Museum of Harvard University
Cambridge, Mass. 02138

The Bromeliad Society
Jeanne Woodbury
1811 Edgecliff Drive
Los Angeles, Calif.

Bromeliad Society Bulletin

Epiphyllum Society of America
Gene Luchenbacher
4400 Portola Avenue
Los Angeles, Calif.

Bulletin

Saintpaulia International
Mrs. Alma Wright
P.O. Box 10604
Knoxville, Tenn. 37919

Gesneriad-Saintpaulia News

Books for Indoor Gardeners

ALL ABOUT MINIATURE PLANTS AND GARDENS, Bernice Brilmayer, New York, Doubleday, 1963.

BEGONIAS, INDOORS AND OUT, Jack Kramer, New York, E. P. Dutton, 1967.

THE BOOK OF CACTI AND OTHER SUCCULENTS, Claude Chidamian, New York, Doubleday, 1958.

BROMELIADS, THE COLORFUL HOUSE PLANTS, Jack Kramer, Princeton, N.J., Van Nostrand, 1965.

THE CITY GARDENER, Philip Truex, New York, Alfred A. Knopf, 1964.

FLOWERING BULBS FOR WINTER WINDOWS, Marion C. Walker, Princeton, N.J., Van Nostrand, 1965.

FLUORESCENT LIGHT GARDENING, Elaine C. Cherry, Princeton, N.J., Van Nostrand, 1965.

FOLIAGE PLANTS FOR INDOOR GARDENING, James Underwood Crockett, New York, Doubleday, 1967.

GARDEN IN YOUR HOUSE, Ernesta Drinker Ballard, New York, Harper, 1958.

GESNERIADS, AND HOW TO GROW THEM, Edited by Peggy Schulz, Kansas City, Mo., Diversity Books, 1967.

GROWING ORCHIDS AT YOUR WINDOWS, Jack Kramer, Princeton, N.J., Van Nostrand, 1963.

THE JOY OF GERANIUMS, Helen Van Pelt Wilson, New York, Barrows, 1967.

MINIATURE PLANTS FOR HOME AND GREENHOUSE, Elvin McDonald, Princeton, N.J., Van Nostrand, 1963.

THE NEW COMPLETE BOOK OF AFRICAN VIOLETS, Helen Van Pelt Wilson, New York, Barrows, 1963.

1001 HOUSE PLANT QUESTIONS ANSWERED, Stanley Schuler, Princeton, N.J., Van Nostrand, 1963.

VARIEGATED FOLIAGE PLANTS, Paul Fischer, London, Blandford Press, 1960.

Where to Buy Plants

Alberts & Merkel Bros., Inc.
P.O. Box 537
Boynton Beach, Fla. 33435

Orchids, bromeliads, and other tropical plants. Catalogue 50¢

Antonelli Bros.
2545 Capitola Road
Santa Crux, Calif. 95010

Gesneriads, begonias.

Ashcroft Orchids
19062 Ballinger Way N.E.
Seattle, Wash. 98155

Species orchids.

Buell's Greenhouses
Eastford, Conn. 06242

Gloxinias African-violets.

Burgess Seed & Plant Co., Inc.
67 E. Battle Creek St.
Galesburg, Mich. 49053

Many kinds of house plants.

W. Atlee Burpee Co.
Philadelphia, Pa. 19132

Seeds and bulbs.

P. De Jager & Sons, Inc.
188 Asbury St.
S. Hamilton, Mass. 01982

Outstanding selection of bulbs.

Fantastic Gardens
9550 S.W. 67th Avenue
South Miami, Fla. 33030

Tropical plants, bromeliads.

Fennell Orchid Co. 26715 S.W. 157 Ave. Homestead, Fla. 33030	Wide selection of orchids. Catalogue 50¢
Fischer Greenhouses Linwood, N.J. 08221	African-violets and other gesneriads.
Hauserman's Orchids Box 363 Elmhurst, Ill. 60218	Wide selection of species orchids.
Margaret Ilgenfritz Box 665 Monroe, Mich. 48161	Large selection of species orchids. Catalogue $1.00
Johnson Cactus Gardens Box 207 Bonsall, Calif. 92003	Cacti and succulents. Mail order only.
Kartuz Greenhouses 92 Chestnut St. Wilmington, Mass. 01887	House plants, especially bromeliads.
Logee's Greenhouses 55 North St. Danielson, Conn. 06239	All kinds of house plants. Catalogue 50¢
Lyndon Lyon 14 Mutchler St. Dolgeville, N.Y. 13329	African-violets, columneas.
Rod McLellan Co. 1450 El Camino Real S. San Francisco, Calif. 94080	Orchids.
Merry Gardens Camden, Maine 04843	Complete selection of house plants. Catalogue $1.00
Oakhurst Gardens P.O. Box 444 Arcadia, Calif. 91008	Unusual bulbs, house plants. Catalogue 50¢
George W. Park Seed Co., Inc. Box 31 Greenwood, S. Carolina 29646	All kinds of house plants, seeds.

Julius Roehrs Co. East Rutherford, N.J. 07073	House plants.
Max Schling, Seedsmen, Inc. 538 Madison Ave. New York, N.Y. 10022	Seeds, bulbs, house plants.
Tinari Greenhouses 2325 Valley Road Bethayres, Pa. 19006	African-violets and other plants.
Tropical Paradise Greenhouses 8825 W. 79th St. Overland Park, Kansas 66200	Wide selection of house plants.
Wilson Bros. Roachdale, Indiana 46172	Geraniums and other house plants.

Where to Buy Supplies

Floralite Co. 4124 E. Oakwood Road Oak Creek, Wis. 53154	All kinds of plant equipment.
The House Plant Corner P.O. Box 810 Oxford, Md. 21654	All kinds of supplies.
George W. Park Seed Co. Box 31 Greenwood, S. Carolina 29646	Lighted plant stands and other equipment.
Harvey J. Ridge 1126 Arthur Street Wausau, Wis. 54401	All kinds of supplies.
Shoplite Co. 650 Franklin Ave. Nutley, N.J. 07110	Artificial light equipment.
Tube Craft, Inc. 1311 W. 80th St. Cleveland, Ohio 44102	Artificial light equipment and other supplies.
Union Products, Inc. 511 Lancaster St. Leominster, Mass. 01453	Miniature greenhouses and accessories.

Words to Know

Bract	Modified leaf near the base of the flower, often colorful as in the poinsettia.
Bulb	Plant structure for storage purposes, usually underground, includes corm, rhizome, and tuber.
Calyx	Outer circle of floral parts, usually green.
Compost	Decomposed vegetable matter.
Cultivar	Plant form originating in cultivation.
Cutting	Vegetative plant part capable of producing identical plant.
Deciduous	Plants that lose leaves at maturity in certain seasons.
Dormant	Resting, a period of inactivity when plants grow less or not at all.
Epiphyte	Plant that grows upon another plant or object but derives no nourishment from it.
Force	To make a plant grow or bloom ahead of its natural season.
Frond	Leaf of a fern or a palm.
Germination	Process of seed sprouting.
Hybrid	Offspring from the crossing of two different species or strains of the same species.
Leaflet	Segment of a compound leaf.
Leafmold	Decayed or decomposed leaves, useful in potting mixes.
Node	Joint on a stem where a bud or leaf is attached.
Ovate	Egg-shaped.
Palmate	Leaf form, like a hand, with radiating veins or leaflets.
Petal	A flower leaf, the colorful part.
Petiole	Supporting stalk of a leaf.
Pinnate	Leaf form, like a feather, with sections arranged along the side of the leaf stalk.
Potbound	Condition of a plant when a mat of roots fills the container.
Raceme	Elongated flower cluster.
Rhizome	Rootlike fleshy stem underground or creeping on soil.
Rosette	A cluster of radiating leaves.
Runner	Vagrant shoot that runs along the ground.
Sepal	Segment of a calyx.
Sphagnum moss	Bog material dried and used alone as a planting medium or in a mixture.
Spike	Elongated flower cluster.
Stolon	Creeping horizontal stem usually producing a new plant at tip.
Succulent	Type of plant that stores moisture in stems or leaves.
Tuber	Fleshy underground branch with buds near the surface.
Umbel	Flat or ball-shaped flower cluster.
Vermiculite	Sterile mica product for rooting plants or including in a soil mixture.

Index

46

1000 Beautiful House Plants and How to Grow Them ...

. . . is the *complete* guide to all the familiar, and many of the unfamiliar, plants for indoor growing. Whether you want an attractive window garden of plants suited to *your* conditions, a plant room filled with color, a fluorescent light set-up, a bottle or dish garden, or winter-into-spring pictures with tender and hardy bulbs, you will find here just the information you need.

In the A to Z Dictionary of botanical and common names, size, foliage, time and color of bloom are given for each plant with requirements of light, soil, and water. How to get months of color from your Thanksgiving cactus, your Christmas poinsettias and cyclamens, weeks from your Easter azaleas (also how to get them all to bloom for you next year), what to do with your Easter lily, and how to bring an amaryllis or a pot of tulips to perfection are explained in detail.

All the old favorites are discussed—begonias, ferns, geraniums, palms, and vines for brackets and baskets—also how to grow orchids at your windows, bromeliads in your hall or office, and how to succeed with African-violets, gloxinias, and other gesneriads. With this book as guide, you can have something in bloom every month in the year, you can discover a world of unusual plants—the fruiting ardisia, the long-flowering true-blue eranthemum, the carmine ruellia, and white plectranthus—the miniatures and the fragrant kinds.

JACK KRAMER has been an enthusiastic indoor gardener for a long time, and he has discovered how to grow a multitude of house plants successfully under such different conditions as a steam-heated Chicago apartment, an enclosed porch in Miami, and a garden room in California. His great enthusiasms are orchids and bromeliads as window plants, but through the years he has run the gamut of the plants in this book. He is the author of close to 20 other gardening books and has contributed garden articles to *Family Circle, Flower & Garden, Horticulture, House Beautiful* and *Popular Gardening.* He is a member of the Bromeliad Society, the American Horticultural Society, the American Begonia Society, the American Orchid Society, and the Garden Writers Association of America.

46 illustrations in color,
73 black-and-white photographs, 3 pages of working drawings

WILLIAM MORROW & COMPANY, INC.
105 Madison Avenue, New York, N.Y. 10016

$5.95

0-688-05843-4